HBR'S 10 MUST READS

The definitive
management ideas
of the year from
Harvard Business Review.

2016

HBR's 10 Must Reads series is the definitive collection of ideas and best practices for aspiring and experienced leaders alike. These books offer essential reading selected from the pages of *Harvard Business Review* on topics critical to the success of every manager.

Titles include:

HBR's 10 Must Reads 2015
HBR's 10 Must Reads 2016
HBR's 10 Must Reads on Change Management
HBR's 10 Must Reads on Collaboration
HBR's 10 Must Reads on Communication
HBR's 10 Must Reads on Emotional Intelligence
HBR's 10 Must Reads on Innovation
HBR's 10 Must Reads on Leadership
HBR's 10 Must Reads on Making Smart Decisions
HBR's 10 Must Reads on Managing People
HBR's 10 Must Reads on Managing Yourself
HBR's 10 Must Reads on Strategic Marketing
HBR's 10 Must Reads on Strategy
HBR's 10 Must Reads on Teams
HBR's 10 Must Reads: The Essentials

The definitive
management ideas
of the year from
Harvard Business Review.

HARVARD BUSINESS REVIEW PRESS
Boston, Massachusetts

Copyright 2016 Harvard Business School Publishing Corporation
All rights reserved
Printed in the United States of America

10 9 8 7 6 5 4 3 2 1

The web addresses referenced in this book were live and correct at the time of the book's publication but may be subject to change.

Cataloging-in-Publication data is forthcoming.

ISBN: 978-1-63369-080-6
eISBN: 978-1-63369-081-3

The paper used in this publication meets the requirements of the American National Standard for Permanence of Paper for Publications and Documents in Libraries and Archives Z39.48-1992.

Contents

Editors' Note

As our editorial team read through the past year's worth of *Harvard Business Review* to select the articles for this volume, perhaps the most interesting part of the proceeding was seeing how a group of seemingly disparate articles actually overlapped and wove together. Of course some themes were the result of deliberate effort; but accidental commonalities and contrasts perhaps even better represent the interests of our authors and our readers. This year we saw organizations focused on their physical spaces, and we've included two articles from our issue on workplaces. But one of them, tellingly, also addresses the issue of privacy in the virtual world, which dovetails with questions raised by the growing internet of things and its attendant business models. That interplay of digital and physical worlds (not to mention innovative business models) is also embodied in the rise of 3-D printing. Among the other themes that emerged were better collaboration through the breaking down of physical walls and organizational silos (But how much of this openness is too much?); the balance between intuition and rationality; and the (im)balance between corporate profit and human prosperity.

This volume begins by focusing on the critical (if more prosaic) process of assessing performance. In **"Reinventing Performance Management,"** Marcus Buckingham and Ashley Goodall describe how Deloitte overhauled its performance management system. In a public survey the company conducted, more than half the executive participants indicated that their current method of evaluating employees' work neither drove employee engagement nor encouraged high performance: It depended too much on past results and offered no practical look into the future. In the new model, rather than asking for their impressions of a particular individual, the performance system asks managers what they would *do* with the employee to recognize, capture, and fuel performance—bringing agility and constant learning into the center of the organization's culture.

In **"The Transparency Trap,"** the Harvard Business School professor Ethan Bernstein takes up the question of performance as well, examining how openness—both in a physical context and through the use of technology and social platforms—can affect a team's creativity and productivity. Companies are increasingly using open environments to encourage idea sharing and accountability. But Bernstein's research shows that too much transparency can stifle experimental behaviors that might benefit the enterprise. Privacy, he finds, is just as essential as transparency for high performance. Bernstein goes on to suggest four types of boundaries to establish zones for private work within transparent organizations.

Shifting away from the individual worker, our next piece focuses on the corporation and how its performance affects the U.S. economy. In his McKinsey Award–winning call to action, **"Profits Without Prosperity,"** William Lazonick, an economics professor at the University of Massachusetts Lowell and a codirector of its Center for Industrial Competitiveness, studies the reasons behind the increasing underpayment—and unemployment—of American workers, despite a booming stock market. Lazonick corrals remarkable research to suggest that executives are using massive stock buybacks to manipulate share prices and boost their own allocation of corporate profits. Rather than contribute further to executive compensation, he argues, companies should reinvest profits in their people for future growth.

On the level of individual managerial skills, **"Outsmart Your Own Biases"** describes some of the toughest traps leaders fall into as they make hard choices—tunnel vision about future scenarios, about objectives, and about options—and encourages them to broaden their perspective. A variety of methods, from premortems to joint evaluations, can help us overcome the habits that prevent good decision making and move beyond gut instinct to deliberate reasoning.

Another prominent theme this year was how technological advances are changing the way businesses compete. One such advance is 3-D printing. Many have already discussed the changes this technology could potentially bring to the manufacturing sector. But as the Dartmouth strategy professor Richard D'Aveni asserts in **"The 3-D Printing Revolution,"** industrial 3-D printing is no longer just about prototyping or creating trinkets and toys. This transformative technology is gaining momentum, and any companies that sell products will be affected—from their internal processes to the competitors they face. D'Aveni's forward-looking piece considers the changing landscape and explains how to adjust your company's strategy to redesign customer offerings, optimize operations, and evolve your business model to fit this new context.

But even when the strategy is right, who's to say it will be implemented properly? The next piece in our volume views that perennial struggle through a practical lens. In **"Why Strategy Execution Unravels—and What to Do About It,"** Donald Sull, Rebecca Homkes, and Charles Sull bust five myths about strategy execution—including what it looks like, who drives it, and why it often fails. (Hint: Silos are part of the problem.) By understanding what's behind successful execution, leaders can seize opportunities that align with their strategy, pinpoint where efforts are stalling, and translate their ideas into results.

We turn again to individual development with **"The Authenticity Paradox."** Authenticity is quickly becoming a key leadership trait, says the INSEAD professor Herminia Ibarra. But for many, remaining "authentic" is an excuse for sticking with what's comfortable—which means leaders don't take the risks necessary for growth and development. Instead they should experiment: By trying out a new role or temporarily feeling "fake," they can develop a personal style that feels right to them and suits the organization's changing needs as well.

Experimentation isn't just for leaders; it's a core component of the innovation process for organizations. But many companies skip rigorous experimentation in favor of intuition, leading (again) to bad decisions. In **"The Discipline of Business Experimentation,"** the authors use examples from Kohl's, Wawa, and Petco to show how companies can effectively test-drive innovation efforts to improve their operations and products. What makes this article important is not the specific questions it asks (although those are valuable) but that it draws from the authors' extensive research and experience to give readers a full understanding of how to try out ideas in the market while minimizing risk.

Innovation, experimentation—they often rely on diverse perspectives and areas of expertise. But what can you do when your best people from various groups and disciplines won't collaborate? Professional services firms often find themselves in just that situation: Partners are so accustomed to competing with one another that they don't work together even for the benefit of a shared client—or of their company. In **"When Senior Managers Won't Collaborate,"** Heidi K. Gardner, who studies legal organizations and other professional services firms, explains how one organization recognized this issue and helped partners with diverse specialties work together to provide a higher-value combined offering for clients, thus growing revenue for the whole firm. Though the piece focuses on professional services, its lessons are applicable to any organization looking to create a more collaborative culture.

A culture of collaboration is also the focus of **"Workspaces That Move People."** Here the authors urge leaders to create physical workplaces that encourage face-to-face communication and chance encounters among employees. On the surface, this may seem to contradict the zones of privacy suggested in "The Transparency Trap." But the authors focus less on visibility and more on spontaneity. They suggest making changes to your physical space that promote informal cross-silo conversation to generate ideas and expand learning. With small tweaks, such as reducing the number of coffee machines, and larger changes, such as increasing the size of break rooms or establishing easily reconfigurable spaces, leaders can orchestrate the unplanned interactions that lead employees to mingle and share knowledge—all for greater creativity and productivity.

It's striking to see how much discussion this year was focused on in-person interaction and collaboration, since so much of work and life is now mediated by digital devices. In **"Digital Ubiquity: How Connections, Sensors, and Data Are Revolutionizing Business,"** the Harvard Business School professors Marco Iansiti and Karim R. Lakhani discuss the competitive landscape created by the internet of things as it connects previously distinct products and services. Using GE as a central example, they show how companies can proactively evolve their business models to stay ahead—and take advantage—of this digital revolution.

From disruptive technological advances to new ways of working together, business is transforming. Some articles we publish in HBR help leaders prepare for the future by describing the here and now—by showing how innovative practices can work in real organizations, for example, or by presenting research that can help them hone their management skills. Others point more explicitly to what's coming. We hope that this volume, in combining both, helps leaders meet the changing competitive landscape head-on.

—The Editors

The definitive
management ideas
of the year from
Harvard Business Review.

2016

Reinventing Performance Management

by Marcus Buckingham and Ashley Goodall

AT DELOITTE WE'RE REDESIGNING our performance management system. This may not surprise you. Like many other companies, we realize that our current process for evaluating the work of our people—and then training them, promoting them, and paying them accordingly—is increasingly out of step with our objectives. In a public survey Deloitte conducted recently, more than half the executives questioned (58%) believe that their current performance management approach drives neither employee engagement nor high performance. They, and we, are in need of something nimbler, real-time, and more individualized—something squarely focused on fueling performance in the future rather than assessing it in the past.

What might surprise you, however, is what we'll include in Deloitte's new system and what we won't. It will have no cascading objectives, no once-a-year reviews, and no 360-degree-feedback tools. We've arrived at a very different and much simpler design for managing people's performance. Its hallmarks are speed, agility, one-size-fits-one, and constant learning, and it's underpinned by a new way of collecting reliable performance data. This system will make much more sense for our talent-dependent business. But we might never have arrived at its design without drawing on three pieces of evidence: a simple counting of hours, a review of research in the science of ratings, and a carefully controlled study of our own organization.

Counting and the Case for Change

More than likely, the performance management system Deloitte has been using has some characteristics in common with yours. Objectives are set for each of our 65,000-plus people at the beginning of the year; after a project is finished, each person's manager rates him or her on how well those objectives were met. The manager also comments on where the person did or didn't excel. These evaluations are factored into a single year-end rating, arrived at in lengthy "consensus meetings" at which groups of "counselors" discuss hundreds of people in light of their peers.

Internal feedback demonstrates that our people like the predictability of this process and the fact that because each person is assigned a counselor, he or she has a representative at the consensus meetings. The vast majority of our people believe the process is fair. We realize, however, that it's no longer the best design for Deloitte's emerging needs: Once-a-year goals are too "batched" for a real-time world, and conversations about year-end ratings are generally less valuable than conversations conducted in the moment about actual performance.

But the need for change didn't crystallize until we decided to count things. Specifically, we tallied the number of hours the organization was spending on performance management—and found that completing the forms, holding the meetings, and creating the ratings consumed close to *2 million hours a year.* As we studied how those hours were spent, we realized that many of them were eaten up by leaders' discussions behind closed doors about the outcomes of the process. We wondered if we could somehow shift our investment of time from talking to ourselves about ratings to talking to our people about their performance and careers—from a focus on the past to a focus on the future.

The Science of Ratings

Our next discovery was that assessing someone's *skills* produces inconsistent data. Objective as I may try to be in evaluating you on, say, strategic thinking, it turns out that how much strategic thinking *I* do, or how valuable *I* think strategic thinking is, or how tough

Idea in Brief

The Problem

Not just employees but their managers and even HR departments are by now questioning the conventional wisdom of performance management, including its common reliance on cascading objectives, backward-looking assessments, once-a-year rankings and reviews, and 360-degree-feedback tools.

The Goal

Some companies have ditched the rankings and even annual reviews, but they haven't found better solutions. Deloitte resolved to design a system that would fairly recognize varying performance, have a clear view into performance anytime, and boost performance in the future.

The Solution

Deloitte's new approach separates compensation decisions from day-to-day performance management, produces better insight through quarterly or per-project "performance snapshots," and relies on weekly check-ins with managers to keep performance on course.

a rater *I* am significantly affects my assessment of *your* strategic thinking.

How significantly? The most comprehensive research on what ratings actually measure was conducted by Michael Mount, Steven Scullen, and Maynard Goff and published in the *Journal of Applied Psychology* in 2000. Their study—in which 4,492 managers were rated on certain performance dimensions by two bosses, two peers, and two subordinates—revealed that 62% of the variance in the ratings could be accounted for by individual raters' peculiarities of perception. Actual performance accounted for only 21% of the variance. This led the researchers to conclude (in *How People Evaluate Others in Organizations,* edited by Manuel London): "Although it is implicitly assumed that the ratings measure the performance of the ratee, most of what is being measured by the ratings is the unique rating tendencies of the rater. Thus ratings reveal more about the rater than they do about the ratee." This gave us pause. We wanted to understand performance at the individual level, and we knew that the person in the best position to judge it was the immediate team leader. But how could we capture a team leader's view of performance without running afoul of what the researchers termed "idiosyncratic rater effects"?

3

Putting Ourselves Under the Microscope

We also learned that the defining characteristic of the very best teams at Deloitte is that they are strengths oriented. Their members feel that they are called upon to do their best work every day. This discovery was not based on intuitive judgment or gleaned from anecdotes and hearsay; rather, it was derived from an empirical study of our own high-performing teams.

Our study built on previous research. Starting in the late 1990s, Gallup performed a multiyear examination of high-performing teams that eventually involved more than 1.4 million employees, 50,000 teams, and 192 organizations. Gallup asked both high- and lower-performing teams questions on numerous subjects, from mission and purpose to pay and career opportunities, and isolated the questions on which the high-performing teams strongly agreed and the rest did not. It found at the beginning of the study that almost all the variation between high- and lower-performing teams was explained by a very small group of items. The most powerful one proved to be "At work, I have the opportunity to do what I do best every day." Business units whose employees chose "strongly agree" for this item were 44% more likely to earn high customer satisfaction scores, 50% more likely to have low employee turnover, and 38% more likely to be productive.

We set out to see whether those results held at Deloitte. First we identified 60 high-performing teams, which involved 1,287 employees and represented all parts of the organization. For the control group, we chose a representative sample of 1,954 employees. To measure the conditions within a team, we employed a six-item survey. When the results were in and tallied, three items correlated best with high performance for a team: "My coworkers are committed to doing quality work," "The mission of our company inspires me," and "I have the chance to use my strengths every day." Of these, the third was the most powerful across the organization.

All this evidence helped bring into focus the problem we were trying to solve with our new design. We wanted to spend more time helping our people use their strengths—in teams characterized by great clarity of purpose and expectations—and we wanted a quick way to collect reliable and differentiated performance data. With this in mind, we set to work.

Radical Redesign

We began by stating as clearly as we could what performance management is actually *for,* at least as far as Deloitte is concerned. We articulated three objectives for our new system. The first was clear: It would allow us to *recognize* performance, particularly through variable compensation. Most current systems do this.

But to recognize each person's performance, we had to be able to *see* it clearly. That became our second objective. Here we faced two issues—the idiosyncratic rater effect and the need to streamline our traditional process of evaluation, project rating, consensus meeting, and final rating. The solution to the former requires a subtle shift in our approach. Rather than asking more people for their opinion of a team member (in a 360-degree or an upward-feedback survey, for example), we found that we will need to ask only the immediate team leader—but, critically, to ask a different kind of question. People may rate other people's skills inconsistently, but they are highly consistent when rating their own feelings and intentions. To see performance at the individual level, then, we will ask team leaders not about the *skills* of each team member but about their *own future actions* with respect to that person.

At the end of every project (or once every quarter for long-term projects) we will ask team leaders to respond to four future-focused statements about each team member. We've refined the wording of these statements through successive tests, and we know that at Deloitte they clearly highlight differences among individuals and reliably measure performance. Here are the four:

1. Given what I know of this person's performance, and if it were my money, I would award this person the highest possible compensation increase and bonus [*measures overall performance and unique value to the organization on a five-point scale from "strongly agree" to "strongly disagree"*].

2. Given what I know of this person's performance, I would always want him or her on my team [*measures ability to work well with others on the same five-point scale*].

3. This person is at risk for low performance [*identifies problems that might harm the customer or the team on a yes-or-no basis*].

4. This person is ready for promotion today [*measures potential on a yes-or-no basis*].

In effect, we are asking our team leaders what they would *do* with each team member rather than what they *think* of that individual. When we aggregate these data points over a year, weighting each according to the duration of a given project, we produce a rich stream of information for leaders' discussions of what they, in turn, will do—whether it's a question of succession planning, development paths, or performance-pattern analysis. Once a quarter the organization's leaders can use the new data to review a targeted subset of employees (those eligible for promotion, for example, or those with critical skills) and can debate what actions Deloitte might take to better develop that particular group. In this aggregation of simple but powerful data points, we see the possibility of shifting our 2-million-hour annual investment from talking about the ratings to talking about our people—from ascertaining the facts of performance to considering what we should do in response to those facts.

In addition to this consistent—and countable—data, when it comes to compensation, we want to factor in some uncountable things, such as the difficulty of project assignments in a given year and contributions to the organization other than formal projects. So the data will serve as the starting point for compensation, not the ending point. The final determination will be reached either by a leader who knows each individual personally or by a group of leaders looking at an entire segment of our practice and at many data points in parallel.

We could call this new evaluation a rating, but it bears no resemblance, in generation or in use, to the ratings of the past. Because it allows us to quickly capture performance at a single moment in time, we call it a *performance snapshot*.

The Third Objective

Two objectives for our new system, then, were clear: We wanted to recognize performance, and we had to be able to see it clearly. But all our research, all our conversations with leaders on the topic of performance management, and all the feedback from our people left us convinced that something was missing. Is performance management at root more about "management" or about "performance"? Put differently, although it may be great to be able to measure and reward the performance you have, wouldn't it be better still to be able to improve it?

Our third objective therefore became to *fuel* performance. And if the performance snapshot was an organizational tool for measuring it, we needed a tool that team leaders could use to strengthen it.

Research into the practices of the best team leaders reveals that they conduct regular check-ins with each team member about near-term work. These brief conversations allow leaders to set expectations for the upcoming week, review priorities, comment on recent work, and provide course correction, coaching, or important new information. The conversations provide clarity regarding what is expected of each team member and why, what great work looks like, and how each can do his or her best work in the upcoming days—in other words, exactly the trinity of purpose, expectations, and strengths that characterizes our best teams.

Our design calls for every team leader to check in with each team member once a week. For us, these check-ins are not *in addition* to the work of a team leader; they *are* the work of a team leader. If a leader checks in less often than once a week, the team member's priorities may become vague and aspirational, and the leader can't be as helpful—and the conversation will shift from coaching for near-term work to giving feedback about past performance. In other words, the content of these conversations will be a direct outcome of their frequency: If you want people to talk about how to do their best work in the near future, they need to talk often. And so far we have found in our testing a direct and measurable correlation between the frequency of these conversations and the engagement of team

Performance intelligence

In an early proof of concept of the redesigned system, executives in one large practice area at Deloitte called up data from project managers to consider important talent-related decisions. In the charts below, each dot represents an individual; decision makers could click on a dot to see the person's name and details from his or her "performance snapshots."

What are team leaders telling us?

*First the group looked at the whole story. This view plotted all the members of the practice according to how much their various project managers agreed with two statements: "I would always want this person on my team" (**y axis**) and "I would give this person the highest possible compensation" (**x axis**). The axes are the same for the other three screens.*

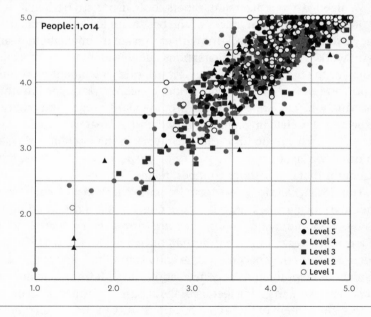

members. Very frequent check-ins (we might say *radically* frequent check-ins) are a team leader's killer app.

That said, team leaders have many demands on their time. We've learned that the best way to ensure frequency is to have check-ins be initiated by the team member—who more often than not is eager for

How would this data help determine pay?

Next the data was filtered to look only at individuals at a given job level. A fundamental question for performance management systems is whether they can capture enough variation among people to fairly allocate pay. A data distribution like this offers a starting point for broader discussion.

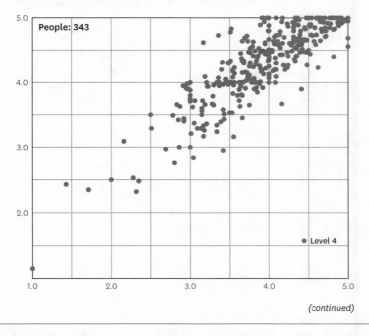

People: 343

Level 4

(continued)

the guidance and attention they provide—rather than by the team leader.

To support both people in these conversations, our system will allow individual members to understand and explore their strengths using a self-assessment tool and then to present those strengths to their teammates, their team leader, and the rest of the organization. Our reasoning is twofold. First, as we've seen, people's strengths generate their highest performance today and the greatest improvement in their performance tomorrow, and so deserve to be a central focus. Second, if we want to see frequent (weekly!) use of our system, we have to think of it as a consumer technology—that is, designed to be simple, quick, and above all engaging to use. Many of the successful

How would it help guide promotions?

This view was filtered to show individuals whose team leaders responded "yes" to the statement "This person is ready for promotion today." The data supports objectivity in annual executive discussions about advancement.

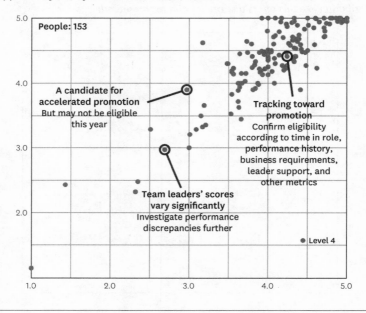

consumer technologies of the past several years (particularly social media) are *sharing* technologies, which suggests that most of us are consistently interested in ourselves—our own insights, achievements, and impact. So we want this new system to provide a place for people to explore and share what is best about themselves.

Transparency

This is where we are today: We've defined three objectives at the root of performance management—to *recognize, see,* and *fuel* performance. We have three interlocking rituals to support them—the annual compensation decision, the quarterly or per-project

How would it help address low performance?

This view was filtered to show individuals whose team leaders responded "yes" to the statement "This person is at risk of low performance." As the upper right of this screen shows, even high performers can slip up—and it's important that the organization help them recover.

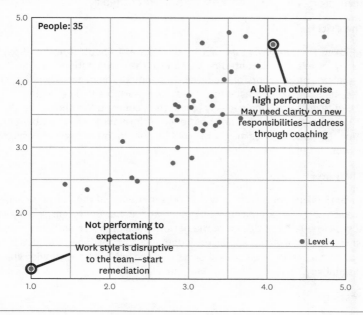

performance snapshot, and the weekly check-in. And we've shifted from a batched focus on the past to a continual focus on the future, through regular evaluations and frequent check-ins. As we've tested each element of this design with ever-larger groups across Deloitte, we've seen that the change can be an evolution over time: Different business units can introduce a strengths orientation first, then more-frequent conversations, then new ways of measuring, and finally new software for monitoring performance. (See the exhibit "Performance intelligence.")

But one issue has surfaced again and again during this work, and that's the issue of transparency. When an organization knows

How Deloitte Built a Radically Simple Performance Measure

ONE OF THE MOST IMPORTANT TOOLS in our redesigned performance management system is the "performance snapshot." It lets us see performance quickly and reliably across the organization, freeing us to spend more time engaging with our people. Here's how we created it.

1. The Criteria

We looked for measures that met three criteria. To neutralize the idiosyncratic rater effect, we wanted raters to rate their own actions, rather than the qualities or behaviors of the ratee. To generate the necessary range, the questions had to be phrased in the extreme. And to avoid confusion, each one had to contain a single, easily understood concept. We chose one about pay, one about teamwork, one about poor performance, and one about promotion. Those categories may or may not be right for other organizations, but they work for us.

2. The Rater

We were looking for someone with vivid experience of the individual's performance and whose subjective judgment we felt was important. We agreed that team leaders are closest to the performance of ratees and, by virtue of their roles, must exercise subjective judgment. We could have included functional managers, or even ratees' peers, but we wanted to start with clarity and simplicity.

3. Testing

We then tested that our questions would produce useful data. Validity testing focuses on their difficulty (as revealed by mean responses) and the

something about us, and that knowledge is captured in a number, we often feel entitled to know it—to know where we stand. We suspect that this issue will need its own radical answer.

In the first version of our design, we kept the results of performance snapshots from the team member. We did this because we knew from the past that when an evaluation is to be shared, the responses skew high—that is, they are sugarcoated. Because we range of responses (as revealed by standard deviations). We knew that if they consistently yielded a tight cluster of "strongly agree" responses, we wouldn't get the differentiation we were looking for. *Construct* validity and *criterion-related* validity are also important. (That is, the questions should collectively test an underlying theory and make it possible to find correlations with outcomes measured in other ways, such as engagement surveys.)

4. Frequency

At Deloitte we live and work in a project structure, so it makes sense for us to produce a performance snapshot at the end of each project. For longer-term projects we've decided that quarterly is the best frequency. Our goal is to strike the right balance between tying the evaluation as tightly as possible to the experience of the performance and not overburdening our team leaders, lest survey fatigue yield poor data.

5. Transparency

We're experimenting with this now. We want our snapshots to reveal the real-time "truth" of what our team leaders think, yet our experience tells us that if they know that team members will see every data point, they may be tempted to sugarcoat the results to avoid difficult conversations. We know that we'll aggregate an individual's snapshot scores into an annual composite. But what, exactly, should we share at year's end? We want to err on the side of sharing more, not less—to aggregate snapshot scores not only for client work but also for internal projects, along with performance metrics such as hours and sales, in the context of a group of peers—so that we can give our people the richest possible view of where they stand. Time will tell how close to that ideal we can get.

wanted to capture unfiltered assessments, we made the responses private. We worried that otherwise we might end up destroying the very truth we sought to reveal.

But what, in fact, is that truth? What do we see when we try to quantify a person? In the world of sports, we have pages of statistics for each player; in medicine, a three-page report each time we get blood work done; in psychometric evaluations, a battery of tests and percentiles. At work, however, at least when it comes to quantifying performance, we try to express the infinite variety and nuance of a human being in a single number.

Surely, however, a better understanding comes from conversations—with your team leader about how you're doing, or between leaders as they consider your compensation or your career. And these conversations are best served not by a single data point but by many. If we want to do our best to tell you where you stand, we must capture as much of your diversity as we can and then talk about it.

We haven't resolved this issue yet, but here's what we're asking ourselves and testing: What's the most detailed view of you that we can gather and share? How does that data support a conversation about your performance? How can we equip our leaders to have insightful conversations? Our question now is not *What is the simplest view of you?* but *What is the richest?*

Over the past few years the debate about performance management has been characterized as a debate about ratings—whether or not they are fair, and whether or not they achieve their stated objectives. But perhaps the issue is different: not so much that ratings fail to convey what the organization knows about each person but that as presented, that knowledge is sadly one-dimensional. In the end, it's not the particular number we assign to a person that's the problem; rather, it's the fact that there *is* a single number. Ratings are a distillation of the truth—and up until now, one might argue, a necessary one. Yet we want our organizations to know us, and we want to know ourselves at work, and that can't be compressed into a single number. We now have the technology to go from a small data version of our people to a big data version of them. As we scale up our new approach across Deloitte, that's the issue we want to solve next.

Originally published in April 2015. Reprint R1504B

The Transparency Trap

by Ethan Bernstein

"TRANSPARENCY" is a watchword in management these days, and it's easy to understand why. After all, if people conduct their work in plain view, won't they be more open and accountable? Won't they flag and fix problems more easily, and share information and their good ideas more freely?

That's certainly what I expected to discover a few years ago, when I went in search of empirical evidence that transparency improves performance in organizations. But through rigorous field research and experiments, and observations by embedded researchers, I learned that it's not that simple. My findings, which complement various studies on open workspaces, suggest that more-transparent environments are not always better. *Privacy* is just as essential for performance.

Here's the paradox: For all that transparency does to drive out wasteful practices and promote collaboration and shared learning, too much of it can trigger distortions of fact and counterproductive inhibitions. Unrehearsed, experimental behaviors sometimes cease altogether. Wide-open workspaces and copious real-time data on how individuals spend their time can leave employees feeling exposed and vulnerable. Being observed changes their conduct. They start going to great lengths to keep what they're doing under wraps, even if they have nothing bad to hide. If executives pick up on signs of covert activity, they instinctively start to monitor employee behavior even more intensely. And that just aggravates the problem.

If all this seems vaguely Orwellian, so did some of the activities I saw in leading companies where intense visibility and tracking were making things worse, not better. For instance, at one of the world's largest mobile phone factories, which is in China and is owned by a global contract manufacturer, the workers on one line were hiding process *improvements* they had made—not just from managers but from their peers on other lines. Why? Because, as one experienced worker explained, "it's most efficient to hide it now and discuss it later. Everyone is happy: They see what they expect to see, and we meet our targets."

This was not an isolated example. In my research, I found that individuals and groups routinely wasted significant resources in an effort to conceal beneficial activities, because they believed that bosses, peers, and external observers who might see them would have "no idea" how to "properly understand" them. Even when everyone involved had only the best of intentions, being observed distorted behavior instead of improving it.

Some organizations, however, had found the sweet spot between privacy and transparency, getting the benefits of both. They used four types of boundaries to establish certain zones of privacy within open environments: They created boundaries around individual teams—zones of attention—to avoid exposing every little action to the scrutiny of a crowd. They drew boundaries between feedback and evaluation—delineating zones of judgment—to avoid politicking and efforts wasted on managing impressions. They set boundaries between decision rights and improvement rights—establishing zones of slack—to avoid driving out tinkering. And they put boundaries around carefully defined periods of experimentation—zones of time—to avoid both too frequent and too infrequent interruptions. Across several studies involving different industries, cultures, and types of work, the companies that had done all this were the ones that consistently got the most innovative, productive, and thoughtful work from their employees.

Idea in Brief

Problem

To get people to be more creative and productive, managers increase transparency with open workspaces and access to real-time data. But too much transparency can leave employees feeling exposed. As a result, they may actively conceal what they're doing—even when making improvements—reducing productivity and, paradoxically, transparency.

Solution

Employees perform better when they can try out new ideas and approaches within certain zones of privacy. Organizations allow them to do that by drawing four types of boundaries: around teams of people (zones of attention), between feedback and evaluation (zones of judgment), between decision rights and improvement rights (zones of slack), and for set periods of experimentation (zones of time).

Benefit

Less-transparent work environments can yield more-transparent employees. And by balancing transparency and privacy, organizations can encourage just the right amount of "deviance" to foster innovative behavior and boost productivity.

Type 1: Boundaries Around Teams

As social media platforms, wearable devices, and other tools for transparency become more advanced, our sense of being "onstage" is growing. And so, in keeping with the sociologist Erving Goffman's insights about interpersonal behavior, we spend more time *acting,* trying to control others' impressions and avoid embarrassment—particularly at work. We cater to our audience, doing what's expected.

That was the case at the Chinese mobile phone factory, which had 14,000 workers. When I began studying that work environment, it seemed like the epitome of transparency: Each floor—roughly the size of a football field, with no walls or other divisions—held as many as 2,000 workers across shifts.

By embedding into the lines five Chinese-born Harvard undergraduate researchers—who worked, ate, and lived alongside the employees, who knew them only as coworkers—I quickly learned that the production teams hid a great deal from observers, despite the open environment. For example, to speed up assembly, workers scanned multiple bar codes into the system at once instead of scanning each one individually after applying it to a metal shield in a phone, as standard operating procedure required. And team members cross-trained on tasks during downtime—it looked like fooling around from the outside—so they could cover for one another when an operator fell behind. There was no ill intent—only a rational calculation about how to be most productive without having to waste time on explanations.

Such subterfuge is problematic for a host of reasons, though, ranging from increased risk of compliance-related defects to a lack of shared learning. To test some basic interventions that might address it, I set up a few field experiments. On one floor, where 32 production lines made similar mobile data cards, I randomly selected four lines on which to experiment, leaving 28 "controls" to work as they always had.

Because one of the experimental lines was very close to a control line, engineering put up a curtain between the two. When it was raised, one of the embedded students overheard a worker say, "Wouldn't it be nice if they hung up curtains all around the line, so we could be completely closed off? We could be so much more productive if they did that." Curious to see if that would be true, I asked engineering to fully encircle each experimental line with the equivalent of a hospital bed curtain. Over the next five months, to my surprise, the lines with curtains were 10% to 15% more productive than the rest, even when I controlled for other influences (such as the Hawthorne effect, whereby subjects improve simply in response to being studied).

By shielding employees from observation, the curtains supported local problem solving, experimentation, and focus. But within the curtains work became much more transparent. Partly for that reason, defects remained extremely low, even as throughput rose. And over time the camaraderie within boundaries made the workers more likely to share—as a group—their privately worked-out solutions with other lines.

Traditionally, people in organizations expect full transparency within teams but not necessarily beyond them. Team boundaries can allow for productive, selective opacities within starkly transparent environments—as was clear at Valve Software, a top PC game developer I studied with Francesca Gino and Bradley Staats. Valve's 400-plus employees are allowed to allocate 100% of their time to projects they feel are valuable to customers. When they collaborate on new products or features, they form teams called cabals and move their desks (which are set on wheels) together into clusters. The office layout is so fluid, with some individuals rolling their desks to different cabals multiple times a week, that Valve even has an internal application to track desk location.

Valve's cabals choose their own workspaces, creating privacy by positioning themselves at a distance from others. Though transparency is high within them, it's moderate at best across the company because of the physical separation and Valve's distaste for managerial oversight. (No one has the role of keeping tabs on the cabals or shuttling information back and forth.) This gives the cabals more freedom to investigate ideas.

When one employee started a cabal to explore how Valve could get into hardware, the team was initially tiny. Had it immediately tried to rally the support of the entire organization of software engineers, the hardware concept might have been dead on arrival—it's hard to persuade lots of people at once to embrace anything new, even at Valve. But acquiring a few followers with whom to experiment and create prototypes was doable. Gradually, the hardware cabal accreted people and resources, gaining scale and momentum. To recruit more people to join it, early members eventually had to tell others what they were up to. In other words, they increased their transparency outside the group—but in their own way and when they were ready.

Is Valve providing an innovative, productive work environment? Its success suggests that it is. In its 18-year existence, Valve has produced a large share of top PC games. According to its founder, Valve has grown sales by more than 50% every year and brought in more revenue per employee than Apple or Microsoft. Its game platform consumes more bandwidth than most countries do. The cabals help the company compete in a market where creativity and rapid prototype and launch capabilities are critical.

Though Valve is an extreme case (and its success is a product of many factors), other firms are similarly fostering innovation and productivity by allowing privacy within team boundaries. For instance, Google doesn't track when and where its engineers spend the 20% of their time that they devote to projects that interest them personally—but they feel transparently accountable to others *within* the self-organized teams in which the work gets done. And that protected 20% time has been credited with the incubation of more than half of Google's current product portfolio, including Gmail, AdSense, Google Talk, Google News, Google Transit, Google Now, and the Google Transparency Report.

Team boundaries have a big impact on performance for service providers as well. In a recent Harvard Business School study, Melissa Valentine and Amy Edmondson show how such boundaries (in their case, counters delimiting small and very fluid groupings of nurses and physicians) improved teamwork and efficiency in a hospital's emergency department. Transparency and accountability among people working within the boundaries increased. As a result, average patient time in the department fell by more than 40%, with no decrease in quality. Remarkably, the department sustained that improvement for over a year (the length of the study) even though its daily patient volume rose by more than 25%.

Although tools for observation (see the sidebar "Tracking Every Move") and collaboration have become more powerful, making it easier for individuals to do much of their work without formal teams to support them, teams are actually proliferating rather than dying off. Longitudinal surveys show that today nearly all *Fortune* 1000 firms have formal team structures, compared with fewer than 20% in 1980. Though a number of factors are driving that trend, my research suggests it has something to do with the value of boundaries. Workers today can tackle problems in cooperation with large networks—and even crowds—of people, but as teams scholar Richard Hackman demonstrated, they frequently do it better on

Tracking Every Move

MANY OF THE SAME COMPANIES that led the digital transformation of industries are also leading the digital transformation of work—allowing managers to observe from a distance far more than they could before.

Even knowledge work can be digitally monitored now. VoloMetrix—a Seattle-based start-up that extracts and analyzes data from company e-mails, calendars, social platforms, and line-of-business operations—provides employees with "people analytics" productivity dashboards based on their own collaboration and activity data or the data of the people they manage.

Of course, all this can feel intrusive—creepy, even—unless employers say what's in it for those being watched. That's how companies persuade consumers to give up personal information—by offering a quid pro quo. Yet for all the rhetoric about the value of utter transparency, there is scant empirical research to support it. So, what value can managers give in exchange for digitally tracking employees? Can they make the work easier or increase its impact? Can they use the data for recognition rather than coercion?

Ambition, a Y Combinator start-up, is trying to make transparency more engaging and less intrusive by reporting performance data as if employees were players on fantasy football teams (the user interface mimics fantasy football). Meanwhile, more individuals are monitoring their own activity through such devices as the Jawbone UP, the Fitbit, and the Nike+ FuelBand, to improve their behavior. Perhaps that will make them more receptive to digital tracking at work, which can yield equally beneficial self-awareness, even if the boss is watching.

Some Examples:

Amazon warehouse employees carry handheld computers that track and optimize every move.

Tesco warehouse workers wear armbands that do the same.

UPS trucks now have sensors that record nearly every action by their drivers.

Harrah's uses RFID technology to track how long it takes the waitstaff to serve drinks to customers.

clearly bounded teams. Boundaries create a focus on "us" and "our work together," liberated from external noise, whether it's unproductive interference or chaotic workflow. No matter what the work is, some observers will increase productivity, but others will undermine it. Whether boundaries are spatial or psychological, they can limit observation to a zone of people. It happens with curtains, cabals, counters—even nominal team boundaries mitigate the pressures of being onstage by keeping the audience small.

Type 2: Boundaries Between Feedback and Evaluation

Organizations are incorporating more and more real-time data—all those electronic bread crumbs we leave behind as we do our work—into performance assessments. In response, employees waste a lot of valuable energy managing impressions. But tools that separate data-informed feedback from the evaluation process help lower people's defenses and put the focus squarely on productivity and problem solving, where you want it.

In general, any information that goes into a formal performance review tends to put people on edge. Nevertheless, most employees are keenly interested in improving their skills. Just look at the popularity of Rypple, a social media platform created to allow members of organizations to give and gather anonymous feedback. (Salesforce.com purchased Rypple within three years of its launch for $60 million. It's now called Work.com.) "You simply had to ask, 'How am I doing at X?'" explains Rypple cofounder Daniel Debow, "and the answers were purely for you." Because only the recipients had access to their feedback, fear of repercussions was removed from the equation. Further, Debow notes, those giving the feedback submitted honest, useful appraisals—with assurance of privacy, they didn't have to worry that candid criticism might damage colleagues' reputations.

Another way of allowing employees to learn from their day-to-day actions without having every little mistake exposed to management is to deliver feedback within a protective bubble. A large U.S. trucking company did this when it installed a DriveCam at the top of each tractor cab's windshield to improve driver safety and performance. The small video camera points both outside and at the driver, gathering and wirelessly transmitting data that analysts can use to flag risky behaviors and prevent accidents. A green light tells the driver that all is well. But during a "G-force event" (any erratic driving incident that causes gravitational force, such as excessive speeding, slamming of brakes, or sudden swerving), the light blinks red and green. If the force is strong enough, the light turns red and the camera stores footage from eight seconds before and four seconds after the event. (On average, each vehicle's DriveCam stores about five minutes' worth of video a month.) The DriveCam also records key metrics, like the truck's speed and location.

A small group of coaches who oversee fleet safety review any events deemed preventable. Only in a situation involving damage or a willful breaking of the law—for instance, failing to use a seat belt or texting while driving—would the coaches share footage with management. And the supervisors who evaluate the truckers aren't privy to the coaching.

When the DriveCams were installed, drivers initially dreaded "being watched by Big Brother." Some got distracted when the red light came on, which made safety worse. But drivers have since warmed to the cams, because they now trust that management won't use the videos to evaluate or reprimand them. As one coach explains, the collaboration is helping drivers "turn bad habits into good habits" and improving their safety record. When coaches look at the footage with drivers, "it really does help," another says. "It changes people's perspectives." Sometimes it's just a simple realization: "Wow, you know, I was following a little too closely."

Type 3: Boundaries Between Decision Rights and Improvement Rights

Managers work hard to clarify decision rights, and for good reason. Spelling out who gets to make which calls helps organizations run more smoothly. It prevents duplicated effort, for example, and decision gridlock. But the empowerment of a select few can leave the other people in the organization feeling voiceless, especially if they aren't explicitly invited to improve systems, processes, roles, and tasks. Employees may withhold their ideas or implement them on the sly. When organizations don't grant improvement rights to those without decision rights, innovation by those who see solutions where others don't—known as productive, or positive, deviance—is effectively squashed in favor of conformity and compliance.

It's important to draw a line between the two kinds of rights, because the people exercising them have different needs. Holders of decision rights benefit from a transparent environment, where "every small fact becomes the subject of careful, scientific investigation," as Frederick Winslow Taylor put it more than a century ago. But while holders of decision rights want perfect visibility, which requires transparency from everyone, that kind of visibility gets in the way of employees' striving to make things better, because it curtails the experimentation necessary for improvements, as seen in the mobile phone factory and other settings.

In fact, a long stream of research tells us that in the presence of others, people do better on repetitive, practiced tasks—what psychologists call dominant responses—but worse on learning tasks that call for creative thinking. The visibility created by transparency conjures up self-consciousness and inhibitions. That's why musicians perform in front of an audience but practice without one—they need privacy to noodle and make discoveries. So, the right level of transparency—and thus oversight—depends on the activity and the observer. While musicians may practice in front of a teacher, that teacher is an invited coach, not a consumer of their work. Technology is making close scrutiny by large audiences of consumers possible to a degree that Taylor could never have imagined, and clear decision rights amplify its effects. If you're under the spotlight in front of such an audience, the last thing you want to do is to make unpracticed improvements while being held to a performance standard. All that transparency can create yearning for a closed door with a sign that says, "I'm in rehearsal!"

Organizations that understand all this are giving employees a reprieve from total transparency in order to make "slack" (excess resources) more productive rather than more scarce. Take Flextronics, a company that Willy Shih, Nina Bilimoria Angelo, and I have studied. By setting up a "moonshine shop," Flextronics has turned its factory floor in Guadalajara into a veritable Legoland for workers. The shop gives employees a place to develop tools and fixtures for their lines in periods of downtime—creative work that imparts a sense of ownership. (Manufacturing companies often facilitate improvement rights in this way.) Made of simple pipes, connectors, and recycled materials, the designs produced in the shop can cost a tenth of what it takes to produce the more complex, specially sourced fixtures provided by vendors. The quality makes IKEA look high-end, but the designs do the job efficiently, safely, and effectively. More important, the shop encourages continual innovation by the operators, creating efficiencies that would otherwise remain in the imagination of workers.

Manufacturers aren't the only organizations that have made slack more productive by protecting improvement rights. Saravanan Kesavan, Bradley Staats, and I saw this happen at the U.S. retailer Belk when it upgraded a mostly manual labor-scheduling system for its 24,000 employees and 300-plus department stores. Belk could have followed the lead of large retailers that have automated nearly all the scheduling tasks, increasing the efficiency of labor with complex algorithms based on minute-by-minute sales figures, real-time weather predictions, activity-based time studies, and other data. But Belk wanted to give its store managers and schedulers the flexibility to account for staffing variations and other local factors, since retail labor is a key driver of customer experience—and, therefore, sales. So its managers chose the simplest form of the technology and allowed local store managers and schedulers to exercise judgment, revising the schedules proposed by the system without having to seek corporate-level approval.

In the early days they revised more than 70% of the scheduling. Now that rate is below 50%—a more efficient, productive range. And while at least one of Belk's competitors recently suffered well-publicized challenges in getting a return on its new fully automated scheduling system, Belk's pilot stores showed a 2% lift in gross profit by the end of 2013, several months after implementing the version that allowed for overrides.

Which employees should be given improvement rights in order to create productive zones of slack? That depends on the organization and its leadership. In a lean environment everyone may be responsible for improvement. But other companies might treat it as an opportunity, not a mandate, perhaps vesting improvement rights in an R&D unit, a heavyweight team of senior managers, or front-line workers. Or an organization might outsource improvements to suppliers, contractors, or consultants. In any case, the assignment of improvement rights both reflects and influences strategy, so leaders must protect them by putting skunkworks activities inside zones of privacy.

Type 4: Boundaries Around Time

Another way to strike the right balance between transparency and privacy is to experiment within limited blocks of time. With this approach, executives give employees more freedom for a specified period, so people can prepare for—and make the most of—their window of privacy.

This type of boundary complements the other three. A company might set up temporary teams for idea gestation, provide a onetime stream of developmental feedback (such as a 360-degree evaluation) that won't make its way into performance reviews, or assign improvement rights to a certain group for a quarter. Some biotech and consulting firms have borrowed the concept of the sabbatical from education and offered employees periods of relatively opaque slack. Googlers often use their 20% time on Fridays.

Tony Lo, the CEO of Giant Bicycles, granted CFO Bonnie Tu time-limited decision-making authority when he asked her to develop a business model to better meet female customers' needs. Lo saw Tu as a perfect leader for this initiative: Her seniority, reputation, and financial acumen gave her the freedom to break the usual rules. Lo—who was used to checking on important projects monthly, weekly, or even daily—left Tu alone for six months, the amount of time he thought it should take to develop and launch the idea. Tu and her team delivered brilliantly: They created a store in Taipei for women only—which reached profitability faster than any other Giant store. It has spawned a number of innovative products and serves as a model for similar stores around the globe.

In the same spirit, several major retailers have supplemented corporate planograms with "flexograms," enabling individual store managers to change how and where they display products in response to customer behavior. While some retailers, like H&M, have made flexograms a standard practice, most limit them to times of year when local customization and ingenuity are likely to maximize sales. They frequently allow experimentation during the December holiday season, for example. CVS put its sun care displays on wheels so that store managers could easily reposition them to take advantage of fast-changing weather and buying trends at specified times during key periods in the summer.

Sir Alex Ferguson, the former manager of the Manchester United football club, who is widely believed to be one of the greatest coaches in history, had an interesting take on transparency and its effects on performance. Though he championed the use of vests fitted with GPS sensors, which allowed analysis just 20 minutes after a training session, he said he would "never criticize a player during a training session. That's where they try the irreverent things that will, and won't, work during a match."

It's an important point: Irreverence increases our willingness to test how we do things and to deviate from the norm. But total transparency heightens the risk that our irreverence will come back to haunt us—and thus has a chilling effect on experimentation. Advanced sensing and tracking technologies make behavior highly visible in real time. How all that information should be used— by individuals, their teams, their supervisors—is a management question, not a technology question. Organizational cultures that foster psychological safety, trust, balanced power dynamics, and collaboration can help. But it's also critical for leaders to mitigate transparency with zones of privacy, enabling just the right amount of deviance to foster innovation and productivity.

Originally published in October 2014. Reprint R1410D

Profits Without Prosperity

by William Lazonick

FIVE YEARS AFTER the official end of the Great Recession, corporate profits are high, and the stock market is booming. Yet most Americans are not sharing in the recovery. While the top 0.1% of income recipients—which include most of the highest-ranking corporate executives—reap almost all the income gains, good jobs keep disappearing, and new employment opportunities tend to be insecure and underpaid.

Corporate profitability is not translating into widespread economic prosperity.

The allocation of corporate profits to stock buybacks deserves much of the blame. Consider the 449 companies in the S&P 500 index that were publicly listed from 2003 through 2012. During that period those companies used 54% of their earnings—a total of $2.4 trillion—to buy back their own stock, almost all through purchases on the open market. Dividends absorbed an additional 37% of their earnings. That left very little for investments in productive capabilities or higher incomes for employees.

The buyback wave has gotten so big, in fact, that even shareholders—the presumed beneficiaries of all this corporate largesse—are getting worried. "It concerns us that, in the wake of the financial crisis, many companies have shied away from investing in the future growth of their companies," Laurence Fink, the chairman and CEO of BlackRock, the world's largest asset manager, wrote in an open letter to corporate America in March. "Too many companies have cut capital expenditure and even increased debt to boost dividends and increase share buybacks."

Why are such massive resources being devoted to stock repurchases? Corporate executives give several reasons, which I will discuss later. But none of them has close to the explanatory power of this simple truth: Stock-based instruments make up the majority of their pay, and in the short term buybacks drive up stock prices. In 2012 the 500 highest-paid executives named in proxy statements of U.S. public companies received, on average, $30.3 million each; 42% of their compensation came from stock options and 41% from stock awards. By increasing the demand for a company's shares, open-market buybacks automatically lift its stock price, even if only temporarily, and can enable the company to hit quarterly earnings per share (EPS) targets.

As a result, the very people we rely on to make investments in the productive capabilities that will increase our shared prosperity are instead devoting most of their companies' profits to uses that will increase their own prosperity—with unsurprising results. Even when adjusted for inflation, the compensation of top U.S. executives has doubled or tripled since the first half of the 1990s, when it was already widely viewed as excessive. Meanwhile, overall U.S. economic performance has faltered.

If the U.S. is to achieve growth that distributes income equitably and provides stable employment, government and business leaders must take steps to bring both stock buybacks and executive pay under control. The nation's economic health depends on it.

From Value Creation to Value Extraction

For three decades I've been studying how the resource allocation decisions of major U.S. corporations influence the relationship between *value creation* and *value extraction,* and how that relationship affects the U.S. economy. From the end of World War II until the late 1970s, a *retain-and-reinvest* approach to resource allocation

Idea in Brief

The Problem

Corporate profitability is not translating into economic prosperity in the United States. Instead of investing profits in innovation and productive capabilities, U.S. executives are spending them on gigantic stock repurchases.

The Research

These buybacks may increase stock prices in the short term, but in the long term they undermine income equality, job stability, and growth. The buybacks mostly serve the interests of executives, much of whose compensation is in the form of stock.

The Solution

Corporations should be banned from repurchasing their shares on the open market. Executives' excessive stock-based pay should be reined in. Workers and taxpayers should be represented on corporate boards. And Congress should reform the tax system so that it rewards value creation, not value extraction.

prevailed at major U.S. corporations. They retained earnings and reinvested them in increasing their capabilities, first and foremost in the employees who helped make firms more competitive. They provided workers with higher incomes and greater job security, thus contributing to equitable, stable economic growth—what I call "sustainable prosperity."

This pattern began to break down in the late 1970s, giving way to a *downsize-and-distribute* regime of reducing costs and then distributing the freed-up cash to financial interests, particularly shareholders. By favoring value extraction over value creation, this approach has contributed to employment instability and income inequality.

As documented by the economists Thomas Piketty and Emmanuel Saez, the richest 0.1% of U.S. households collected a record 12.3% of all U.S. income in 2007, surpassing their 11.5% share in 1928, on the eve of the Great Depression. In the financial crisis of 2008–2009, their share fell sharply, but it has since rebounded, hitting 11.3% in 2012.

Since the late 1980s, the largest component of the income of the top 0.1% has been compensation, driven by stock-based pay. Meanwhile, the growth of workers' wages has been slow and sporadic, except during the internet boom of 1998–2000, the only time in the past 46 years when real wages rose by 2% or more for three

When productivity and wages parted ways

From 1948 to the mid-1970s, increases in productivity and wages went hand in hand. Then a gap opened between the two.

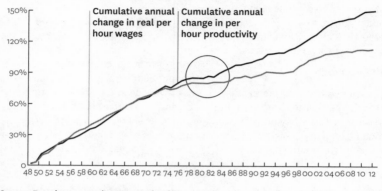

Source: Econdataus.com/Wagegap12.html

years running. Since the late 1970s, average growth in real wages has increasingly lagged productivity growth. (See the exhibit "When productivity and wages parted ways.")

Not coincidentally, U.S. employment relations have undergone a transformation in the past three decades. Mass plant closings eliminated millions of unionized blue-collar jobs. The norm of a white-collar worker's spending his or her entire career with one company disappeared. And the seismic shift toward offshoring left all members of the U.S. labor force—even those with advanced education and substantial work experience—vulnerable to displacement.

To some extent these structural changes could be justified initially as necessary responses to changes in technology and competition. In the early 1980s permanent plant closings were triggered by the inroads superior Japanese manufacturers had made in consumer-durable and capital-goods industries. In the early 1990s one-company careers fell by the wayside in the IT sector because the open-systems architecture of the microelectronics revolution devalued the skills of older employees versed in proprietary technologies. And in the early 2000s the offshoring of more-routine tasks, such as writing unsophisticated software and manning customer call centers, sped up as a capable labor force emerged in low-wage developing economies and communications costs plunged, allowing U.S. companies to focus their domestic employees on higher-value-added work.

These practices chipped away at the loyalty and dampened the spending power of American workers, and often gave away key competitive capabilities of U.S. companies. Attracted by the quick financial gains they produced, many executives ignored the long-term effects and kept pursuing them well past the time they could be justified.

A turning point was the wave of hostile takeovers that swept the country in the 1980s. Corporate raiders often claimed that the complacent leaders of the targeted companies were failing to maximize returns to shareholders. That criticism prompted boards of directors to try to align the interests of management and shareholders by making stock-based pay a much bigger component of executive compensation.

Given incentives to maximize shareholder value and meet Wall Street's expectations for ever higher quarterly EPS, top executives turned to massive stock repurchases, which helped them "manage" stock prices. The result: Trillions of dollars that could have been spent on innovation and job creation in the U.S. economy over the past three decades have instead been used to buy back shares for what is effectively stock-price manipulation.

Good Buybacks and Bad

Not all buybacks undermine shared prosperity. There are two major types: tender offers and open-market repurchases. With the former, a company contacts shareholders and offers to buy back their shares at a stipulated price by a certain near-term date, and then shareholders who find the price agreeable tender their shares to the company. Tender offers can be a way for executives who have substantial ownership stakes and care about a company's long-term competitiveness to take advantage of a low stock price and concentrate ownership in their own hands. This can, among other things, free them from Wall Street's pressure to maximize short-term profits and allow them to invest in the business. Henry Singleton was known for using tender offers in this way at Teledyne in the 1970s, and Warren Buffett for using them at GEICO in the 1980s. (GEICO became wholly owned by Buffett's holding company, Berkshire Hathaway, in 1996.) As Buffett has noted, this kind of tender offer should be made when the share price is below the intrinsic value of the productive capabilities of the company and the company is profitable enough to repurchase the shares without impeding its real investment plans.

But tender offers constitute only a small portion of modern buybacks. Most are now done on the open market, and my research shows that they often come at the expense of investment in productive capabilities and, consequently, aren't great for long-term shareholders.

Companies have been allowed to repurchase their shares on the open market with virtually no regulatory limits since 1982, when the SEC instituted Rule 10b-18 of the Securities Exchange Act. Under the rule, a corporation's board of directors can authorize senior executives to repurchase up to a certain dollar amount of stock over a specified or open-ended period of time, and the company must publicly announce the buyback program. After that, management can buy a large number of the company's shares on any given business day without fear that the SEC will charge it with stock-price manipulation—provided, among other things, that the amount does not exceed a "safe harbor" of 25% of the previous four weeks' average daily trading volume. The SEC requires companies to report total quarterly repurchases but not daily ones, meaning that it cannot determine whether a company has breached the 25% limit without a special investigation.

Despite the escalation in buybacks over the past three decades, the SEC has only rarely launched proceedings against a company for using them to manipulate its stock price. And even within the 25% limit, companies can still make huge purchases: Exxon Mobil, by far the biggest stock repurchaser from 2003 to 2012, can buy back about $300 million worth of shares a day, and Apple up to $1.5 billion a day. In essence, Rule 10b-18 legalized stock market manipulation through open-market repurchases.

The rule was a major departure from the agency's original mandate, laid out in the Securities Exchange Act in 1934. The act was a reaction to a host of unscrupulous activities that had fueled speculation in the Roaring '20s, leading to the stock market crash of 1929 and the Great Depression. To prevent such shenanigans, the act gave the SEC broad powers to issue rules and regulations.

During the Reagan years, the SEC began to roll back those rules. The commission's chairman from 1981 to 1987 was John Shad, a former vice chairman of E.F. Hutton and the first Wall Street insider to lead the commission in 50 years. He believed that the deregulation of securities markets would channel savings into economic investments more efficiently and that the isolated cases of fraud and manipulation that might go undetected did not justify onerous disclosure requirements for companies. The SEC's adoption of Rule 10b-18 reflected that point of view.

Debunking the Justifications for Buybacks

Executives give three main justifications for open-market repurchases. Let's examine them one by one.

1. Buybacks are investments in our undervalued shares that signal our confidence in the company's future.

This makes some sense. But the reality is that over the past two decades major U.S. companies have tended to do buybacks in bull markets and cut back on them, often sharply, in bear markets. (See the exhibit "Where did the money from productivity increases go?") They buy high and, if they sell at all, sell low. Research by the Academic-Industry Research Network, a nonprofit I cofounded and lead, shows that companies that do buybacks never resell the shares at higher prices.

Once in a while a company that bought high in a boom has been forced to sell low in a bust to alleviate financial distress. GE, for example, spent $3.2 billion on buybacks in the first three quarters of

Where did the money from productivity increases go?

Buybacks—as well as dividends—have skyrocketed in the past 20 years. (Note that these data are for the 251 companies that were in the S&P 500 in January 2013 and were public from 1981 through 2012. Inclusion of firms that went public after 1981, such as Microsoft, Cisco, Amgen, Oracle, and Dell, would make the increase in buybacks even more marked.) Though executives say they repurchase only undervalued stocks, buybacks increased when the stock market boomed, casting doubt on that claim.

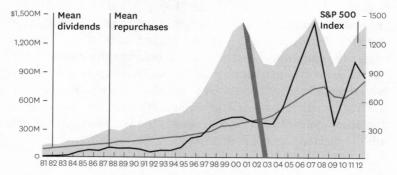

Source: Standard & Poor's Compustat database; the Academic-Industry Research Network.
Note: Mean repurchase and dividend amounts are in 2012 dollars.

2008, paying an average price of $31.84 per share. Then, in the last quarter, as the financial crisis brought about losses at GE Capital, the company did a $12 billion stock issue at an average share price of $22.25, in a failed attempt to protect its triple-A credit rating.

In general, when a company buys back shares at what turn out to be high prices, it eventually reduces the value of the stock held by continuing shareholders. "The *continuing* shareholder is penalized by repurchases above intrinsic value," Warren Buffett wrote in his 1999 letter to Berkshire Hathaway shareholders. "Buying dollar bills for $1.10 is not good business for those who stick around."

2. Buybacks are necessary to offset the dilution of earnings per share when employees exercise stock options.

Calculations that I have done for high-tech companies with broad-based stock option programs reveal that the volume of open-market repurchases is generally a multiple of the volume of options that employees exercise. In any case, there's no logical economic rationale for doing repurchases to offset dilution from the exercise of employee stock options. Options are meant to motivate employees to work harder now to produce higher future returns for the company. Therefore, rather than using corporate cash to boost EPS immediately, executives should be willing to wait for the incentive to work. If the company generates higher earnings, employees can exercise their options at higher stock prices, and the company can allocate the increased earnings to investment in the next round of innovation.

3. Our company is mature and has run out of profitable investment opportunities; therefore, we should return its unneeded cash to shareholders.

Some people used to argue that buybacks were a more tax-efficient means of distributing money to shareholders than dividends. But that has not been the case since 2003, when the tax rates on long-term capital gains and qualified dividends were made the same. Much more important issues remain, however: What is the CEO's main role and his or her responsibility to shareholders?

Companies that have built up productive capabilities over long periods typically have huge organizational and financial advantages when they enter related markets. One of the chief functions of top executives is to discover new opportunities for those capabilities. When they opt to do large open-market repurchases instead, it raises the question of whether these executives are doing their jobs.

A related issue is the notion that the CEO's main obligation is to shareholders. It's based on a misconception of the shareholders' role in the modern corporation. The philosophical justification for giving them all excess corporate profits is that they are best positioned to allocate resources because they have the most interest in ensuring that capital generates the highest returns. This proposition is central to the "maximizing shareholder value" (MSV) arguments espoused over the years, most notably by Michael C. Jensen. The MSV school also posits that companies' so-called free cash flow should be distributed to shareholders because only they make investments without a guaranteed return—and hence bear risk.

But the MSV school ignores other participants in the economy who bear risk by investing without a guaranteed return. *Taxpayers* take on such risk through government agencies that invest in infrastructure and knowledge creation. And *workers* take it on by investing in the development of their capabilities at the firms that employ them. As risk bearers, taxpayers, whose dollars support business enterprises, and workers, whose efforts generate productivity improvements, have claims on profits that are at least as strong as the shareholders'.

The irony of MSV is that public-company shareholders typically never invest in the value-creating capabilities of the company at all. Rather, they invest in outstanding shares in the hope that the stock price will rise. And a prime way in which corporate executives fuel that hope is by doing buybacks to manipulate the market. The only money that Apple ever raised from public shareholders was $97 million at its IPO in 1980. Yet in recent years, hedge fund activists such as David Einhorn and Carl Icahn—who played absolutely no role in the company's success over the decades—have purchased large amounts of Apple stock and then pressured the company to announce some of the largest buyback programs in history.

The past decade's huge increase in repurchases, in addition to high levels of dividends, have come at a time when U.S. industrial companies face new competitive challenges. This raises questions about how much of corporate cash flow is really "free" to be distributed to shareholders. Many academics—for example, Gary P. Pisano and Willy C. Shih of Harvard Business School, in their 2009 HBR article "Restoring American Competitiveness" and their book *Producing Prosperity*— have warned that if U.S. companies don't start investing much more in research and manufacturing capabilities, they cannot expect to remain competitive in a range of advanced technology industries.

Retained earnings have always been the foundation for investments in innovation. Executives who subscribe to MSV are thus copping out of their responsibility to invest broadly and deeply in the productive capabilities their organizations need to continually innovate. MSV as commonly understood is a theory of value extraction, not value creation.

Why money for reinvestment has dried up

Since the early 1980s, when restrictions on open-market buybacks were greatly eased, distributions to shareholders have absorbed a huge portion of net income, leaving much less for reinvestment in companies.

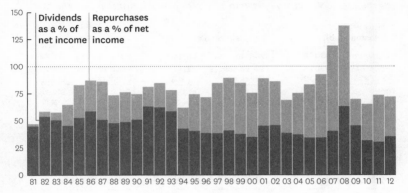

Note: Data are for the 251 companies that were in the S&P 500 Index in January 2013 and were publicly listed from 1981 through 2012. If the companies that went public after 1981, such as Microsoft, Cisco, Amgen, Oracle, and Dell, were included, repurchases as a percentage of net income would be even higher.

Executives Are Serving Their Own Interests

As I noted earlier, there is a simple, much more plausible explanation for the increase in open-market repurchases: the rise of stock-based pay. Combined with pressure from Wall Street, stock-based incentives make senior executives extremely motivated to do buybacks on a colossal and systemic scale.

Consider the 10 largest repurchasers, which spent a combined $859 billion on buybacks, an amount equal to 68% of their combined net income, from 2003 through 2012. (See the exhibit "The top 10 stock repurchasers: 2003–2012.") During the same decade, their CEOs received, on average, a total of $168 million each in compensation. On average, 34% of their compensation was in the form of stock options and 24% in stock awards. At these companies the next four highest-paid senior executives each received, on average, $77 million in

The top 10 stock repurchasers: 2003–2012

At most of the leading U.S. companies below, distributions to shareholders were well in excess of net income. These distributions came at great cost to innovation, employment, and—in cases such as oil refining and pharmaceuticals—customers who had to pay higher prices for products.

#1 Exxon Mobil		#2 Microsoft		#3 IBM	
Net income	**$347B**	Net income	**$148B**	Net income	**$117B**
Repurchases	**$207B**	Repurchases	**$114B**	Repurchases	**$107B**
Dividends	**$80B**	Dividends	**$71B**	Dividends	**$23B**
Total	**$287B**	Total	**$185B**	Total	**$130B**
	83% of NI		125% of NI		111% of NI
CEO pay	**$289B**	CEO pay	**$12M**	CEO pay	**$247M**
% Stock based	73%	% Stock based	0%	% Stock based	64%
	$211M		**$0***		**$158M**

#4 Cisco Systems		#5 Procter & Gamble		#6 Hewlett-Packard	
Net income	**$64B**	Net income	**$93B**	Net income	**$41B**
Repurchases	**$75B**	Repurchases	**$66B**	Repurchases	**$64B**
Dividends	**$2B**	Dividends	**$42B**	Dividends	**$9B**
Total	**$77B**	Total	**$108B**	Total	**$73B**
	121% of NI		116% of NI		177% of NI
CEO pay	**$297M**	CEO pay	**$90M**	CEO pay	**$210M**
% Stock based	92%	% Stock based	16%	% Stock based	37%
	$273M		**$14M**		**$78M**

compensation during the 10 years—27% of it in stock options and 29% in stock awards. Yet since 2003 only three of the 10 largest repurchasers—Exxon Mobil, IBM, and Procter & Gamble—have out-performed the S&P 500 Index.

Reforming the System

Buybacks have become an unhealthy corporate obsession. Shifting corporations back to a retain-and-reinvest regime that promotes stable and equitable growth will take bold action. Here are three proposals.

#7 Walmart	
Net income	**$134B**
Repurchases	**$62B**
Dividends	**$35B**
Total	**$97B**
	73% of NI
CEO pay	**$189M**
% Stock based	62%
	$117M

#8 Intel	
Net income	**$79B**
Repurchases	**$60B**
Dividends	**$27B**
Total	**$87B**
	109% of NI
CEO pay	**$127M**
% Stock based	62%
	$79M

#9 Pfizer	
Net income	**$84B**
Repurchases	**$59B**
Dividends	**$63B**
Total	**$122B**
	146% of NI
CEO pay	**$91M**
% Stock based	25%
	$23M

#10 General Electric	
Net income	**$165B**
Repurchases	**$45B**
Dividends	**$87B**
Total	**$132B**
	81% of NI
CEO pay	**$126M**
% Stock based	25%
	$32M

Sources: Standard & Poor's Compustat Database; Standard & Poor's Execucomp Database; the Academic-Industry Research Network.

Note: The percentages of stock-based pay include gains realized from exercising stock options for all years plus, for 2003–2005, the fair value of restricted stock grants or, for 2006–2012, gains realized on vesting of stock awards. Rounding to the nearest billion may affect total distributions and percentages of net income.

*Steven Ballmer, Microsoft's CEO from January 2000 to February 2014, did not receive any stock-based pay. He does, however, own about 4% of Microsoft's shares, valued at more than $13 billion.

Put an end to open-market buybacks

In a 2003 update to Rule 10b-18, the SEC explained: "It is not appropriate for the safe harbor to be available when the issuer has a heightened incentive to manipulate its share price." In practice, though, the stock-based pay of the executives who decide to do repurchases provides just this "heightened incentive." To correct this glaring problem, the SEC should rescind the safe harbor.

A good first step toward that goal would be an extensive SEC study of the possible damage that open-market repurchases have done to capital formation, industrial corporations, and the U.S. economy over the past three decades. For example, during that period the amount of stock taken out of the market has exceeded the amount issued in almost every year; from 2004 through 2013 this net withdrawal averaged $316 billion a year. In aggregate, the stock market is not functioning as a source of funds for corporate investment. As I've already noted, retained earnings have always provided the base for such investment. I believe that the practice of tying executive compensation to stock price is undermining the formation of physical and human capital.

Rein in stock-based pay

Many studies have shown that large companies tend to use the same set of consultants to benchmark executive compensation, and that each consultant recommends that the client pay its CEO well above average. As a result, compensation inevitably ratchets up over time. The studies also show that even declines in stock price increase executive pay: When a company's stock price falls, the board stuffs even more options and stock awards into top executives' packages, claiming that it must ensure that they won't jump ship and will do whatever is necessary to get the stock price back up.

In 1991 the SEC began allowing top executives to keep the gains from immediately selling stock acquired from options. Previously, they had to hold the stock for six months or give up any "short-swing" gains. That decision has only served to reinforce top executives' overriding personal interest in boosting stock prices. And because corporations aren't required to disclose daily buyback activity, it gives executives the opportunity to trade, undetected, on inside information about when buybacks are being done. At the very least, the SEC should stop allowing executives to sell stock immediately after options are exercised. Such a rule could help launch a much-needed discussion of meaningful reform that goes beyond the 2010 Dodd-Frank Act's "Say on Pay"—an ineffectual law that gives shareholders the right to make nonbinding recommendations to the board on compensation issues.

But overall the use of stock-based pay should be severely limited. Incentive compensation should be subject to performance criteria that reflect investment in innovative capabilities, not stock performance.

Transform the boards that determine executive compensation
Boards are currently dominated by other CEOs, who have a strong bias toward ratifying higher pay packages for their peers. When approving enormous distributions to shareholders and stock-based pay for top executives, these directors believe they're acting in the interests of shareholders.

That's a big part of the problem. The vast majority of shareholders are simply investors in outstanding shares who can easily sell their stock when they want to lock in gains or minimize losses. As I argued earlier, the people who truly invest in the productive capabilities of corporations are taxpayers and workers. Taxpayers have an interest in whether a corporation that uses government investments can generate profits that allow it to pay taxes, which constitute the taxpayers' returns on those investments. Workers have an interest in whether the company will be able to generate profits with which it can provide pay increases and stable career opportunities.

It's time for the U.S. corporate governance system to enter the 21st century: Taxpayers and workers should have seats on boards. Their representatives would have the insights and incentives to ensure that executives allocate resources to investments in capabilities most likely to generate innovations and value.

Courage in Washington

After the Harvard Law School dean Erwin Griswold published "Are Stock Options Getting out of Hand?" in this magazine in 1960, Senator Albert Gore launched a campaign that persuaded Congress to whittle away special tax advantages for executive stock options. After the Tax Reform Act of 1976, the compensation expert Graef Crystal declared that stock options that qualified for the capital-gains tax rate, "once the most popular of all executive compensation devices...have been given the last rites by Congress." It also happens that during the 1970s the share of all U.S. income that the top 0.1% of households got was at its lowest point in the past century.

The members of the U.S. Congress should show the courage and independence of their predecessors and go beyond "Say on Pay" to do something about excessive executive compensation. In addition, Congress should fix a broken tax regime that frequently rewards value extractors as if they were value creators and ignores the critical role of government investment in the infrastructure and knowledge that are so crucial to the competitiveness of U.S. business.

Instead, what we have now are corporations that lobby—often successfully—for federal subsidies for research, development, and exploration, while devoting far greater resources to stock buybacks. Here are three examples of such hypocrisy:

Alternative energy

Exxon Mobil, while receiving about $600 million a year in U.S. government subsidies for oil exploration (according to the Center for American Progress), spends about $21 billion a year on buybacks. It spends virtually no money on alternative energy research.

Meanwhile, through the American Energy Innovation Council, top executives of Microsoft, GE, and other companies have lobbied the U.S. government to triple its investment in alternative energy research and subsidies, to $16 billion a year. Yet these companies had plenty of funds they could have invested in alternative energy on their own. Over the past decade Microsoft and GE, combined, have spent about that amount annually on buybacks.

Nanotechnology

Intel executives have long lobbied the U.S. government to increase spending on nanotechnology research. In 2005, Intel's then-CEO, Craig R. Barrett, argued that "it will take a massive, coordinated U.S. research effort involving academia, industry, and state and federal governments to ensure that America continues to be the world leader in information technology." Yet from 2001, when the U.S. government launched the National Nanotechnology Initiative (NNI), through 2013 Intel's expenditures on buybacks were almost four times the total NNI budget.

Pharmaceutical drugs

In response to complaints that U.S. drug prices are at least twice those in any other country, Pfizer and other U.S. pharmaceutical companies have argued that the profits from these high prices—enabled by a generous intellectual-property regime and lax price regulation—permit more R&D to be done in the United States than elsewhere. Yet from 2003 through 2012, Pfizer funneled an amount equal to 71% of its profits into buybacks, and an amount equal to 75% of its profits into dividends. In other words, it spent more on buybacks and dividends than it earned and tapped its capital reserves to help fund them. The reality is, Americans pay high drug prices so that major pharmaceutical companies can boost their stock prices and pad executive pay.

Given the importance of the stock market and corporations to the economy and society, U.S. regulators must step in to check the behavior of those who are unable or unwilling to control themselves. "The mission of the U.S. Securities and Exchange Commission," the SEC's website explains, "is to protect investors, maintain fair, orderly, and efficient markets, and facilitate capital formation." Yet, as we have seen, in its rulings on and monitoring of stock buybacks and executive pay over three decades, the SEC has taken a course of action contrary to those objectives. It has enabled the wealthiest 0.1% of society, including top executives, to capture the lion's share of the gains of U.S. productivity growth while the vast majority of Americans have been left behind. Rule 10b-18, in particular, has facilitated a rigged stock market that, by permitting the massive distribution of corporate cash to shareholders, has undermined capital formation, including human capital formation.

The corporate resource allocation process is America's source of economic security or insecurity, as the case may be. If Americans want an economy in which corporate profits result in shared prosperity, the buyback and executive compensation binges will have to end. As with any addiction, there will be withdrawal pains. But the best executives may actually get satisfaction out of being paid a reasonable salary for allocating resources in ways that sustain the enterprise, provide higher standards of living to the workers who make it succeed, and generate tax revenues for the governments that provide it with crucial inputs.

Originally published in September 2014. Reprint R1409B

Outsmart Your Own Biases

by Jack B. Soll, Katherine L. Milkman, and John W. Payne

SUPPOSE YOU'RE EVALUATING a job candidate to lead a new office in a different country. On paper this is by far the most qualified person you've seen. Her responses to your interview questions are flawless. She has impeccable social skills. Still, something doesn't feel right. You can't put your finger on what—you just have a sense. How do you decide whether to hire her?

You might trust your intuition, which has guided you well in the past, and send her on her way. That's what most executives say they'd do when we pose this scenario in our classes on managerial decision making. The problem is, unless you occasionally go against your gut, you haven't put your intuition to the test. You can't really know it's helping you make good choices if you've never seen what happens when you ignore it.

It can be dangerous to rely too heavily on what experts call System 1 thinking—automatic judgments that stem from associations stored in memory—instead of logically working through the information that's available. No doubt, System 1 is critical to survival. It's what makes you swerve to avoid a car accident. But as the psychologist Daniel Kahneman has shown, it's also a common source of bias that can result in poor decision making, because our intuitions frequently lead us astray. Other sources of bias involve flawed System 2 thinking—essentially, deliberate reasoning gone awry. Cognitive limitations or laziness, for example, might cause people to focus intently on the wrong things or fail to seek out relevant information.

We are all susceptible to such biases, especially when we're fatigued, stressed, or multitasking. Just think of a CEO who's negotiating a merger while also under pressure from lawyers to decide on a plant closing and from colleagues to manage layoffs. In situations like this, we're far from decision-ready—we're mentally, emotionally, and physically spent. We cope by relying even more heavily on intuitive, System 1 judgments and less on careful reasoning. Decision making becomes faster and simpler, but quality often suffers.

One solution is to delegate and to fight bias at the organizational level, using choice architecture to modify the environment in which decisions are made. Much of the time, though, delegation isn't appropriate, and it's all on you, the manager, to decide. When that's the case, you can outsmart your own biases. You start by understanding where they're coming from: excessive reliance on intuition, defective reasoning, or both. In this article, we describe some of the most stubborn biases out there: tunnel vision about future scenarios, about objectives, and about options. But awareness alone isn't enough, as Kahneman, reflecting on his own experiences, has pointed out. So we also provide strategies for overcoming biases, gleaned from the latest research on the psychology of judgment and decision making.

First, though, let's return to that candidate you're considering. Perhaps your misgivings aren't really about her but about bigger issues you haven't yet articulated. What if the business environment in the new region isn't as promising as forecast? What if employees have problems collaborating across borders or coordinating with the main office? Answers to such questions will shape decisions to scale back or manage continued growth, depending on how the future unfolds. So you should think through contingencies now, when deciding whom to hire.

But asking those bigger, tougher questions does not come naturally. We're cognitive misers—we don't like to spend our mental energy entertaining uncertainties. It's easier to seek closure, so

Idea in Brief

The Problem

Cognitive biases muddy our decision making. We rely too heavily on intuitive, automatic judgments, and even when we try to use reason, our logic is often lazy or flawed.

The Cause

Instead of exploring risks and uncertainties, we seek closure—

it's much easier. This narrows our thinking about what could happen in the future, what our goals are, and how we might achieve them.

The Solution

By knowing which biases tend to trip us up and using certain tricks and tools to outsmart them, we can broaden our thinking and make better choices.

we do. This hems in our thinking, leading us to focus on *one possible future* (in this case, an office that performs as projected), *one objective* (hiring someone who can manage it under those circumstances), and *one option in isolation* (the candidate in front of us). When this narrow thinking weaves a compelling story, System 1 kicks in: Intuition tells us, prematurely, that we're ready to decide, and we venture forth with great, unfounded confidence. To "debias" our decisions, it's essential to broaden our perspective on all three fronts.

Thinking About the Future

Nearly everyone thinks too narrowly about possible outcomes. Some people make one best guess and stop there ("If we build this factory, we will sell 100,000 more cars a year"). Others at least try to hedge their bets ("There is an 80% chance we will sell between 90,000 and 110,000 more cars").

Unfortunately, most hedging is woefully inadequate. When researchers asked hundreds of chief financial officers from a variety of industries to forecast yearly returns for the S&P 500 over a nine-year horizon, their 80% ranges were right only one-third of the time. That's a terribly low rate of accuracy for a group of executives with presumably vast knowledge of the U.S. economy. Projections are even further off the mark when people assess their own plans, partly because their desire to succeed skews their interpretation of the data. (As former Goldman Sachs CFO David Viniar once put it, "The lesson you always learn is that your definition of extreme is not extreme enough.")

Because most of us tend to be highly overconfident in our estimates, it's important to "nudge" ourselves to allow for risk and uncertainty. The following methods are especially useful.

Make three estimates

What will be the price of crude oil in January 2017? How many new homes will be built in the United States next year? How many memory chips will your customers order next month? Such forecasts shape decisions about whether to enter a new market, how many people to hire, and how many units to produce. To improve your accuracy, work up at least three estimates—low, medium, and high—instead of just stating a range. People give wider ranges when they think about their low and high estimates separately, and coming up with three numbers prompts you to do that.

Your low and high guesses should be unlikely but still within the realm of possibility. For example, on the low end, you might say, "There's a 10% chance that we'll sell fewer than 10,000 memory chips next month." And on the high end, you might foresee a 10% chance that sales will exceed 50,000. With this approach, you're less likely to get blindsided by events at either extreme—and you can plan for them. (How will you ramp up production if demand is much higher than anticipated? If it's lower, how will you deal with excess inventory and keep the cash flowing?) Chances are, your middle estimate will bring you closer to reality than a two-number range would.

Think twice

A related exercise is to make two forecasts and take the average. For instance, participants in one study made their best guesses about dates in history, such as the year the cotton gin was invented. Then, asked to assume that their first answer was wrong, they guessed again. Although one guess was generally no closer than the other, people could harness the "wisdom of the inner crowd" by averaging their guesses; this strategy was more accurate than relying on either estimate alone. Research also shows that when people think more than once about a problem, they often come at it with a different perspective, adding valuable information. So tap your own inner crowd and allow time for reconsideration: Project an outcome, take a break (sleep on it if you can), and then come back and project another. Don't refer to your previous estimate—you'll only anchor yourself and limit your ability to achieve new insights. If you can't avoid thinking about your previous estimate, then assume it was wrong and consider reasons that support a different guess.

Use premortems

In a postmortem, the task is typically to understand the cause of a past failure. In a *premortem,* you imagine a future failure and then explain the cause. This technique, also called prospective hindsight, helps you identify potential problems that ordinary foresight won't bring to mind. If you're a manager at an international retailer, you might say: "Let's assume it's 2025, and our Chinese outlets have lost money every year since 2015. Why has that happened?"

Thinking in this way has several benefits. First, it tempers optimism, encouraging a more realistic assessment of risk. Second, it helps you prepare backup plans and exit strategies. Third, it can highlight factors that will influence success or failure, which may increase your ability to control the results.

Perhaps Home Depot would have benefited from a premortem before deciding to enter China. By some accounts, the company was forced to close up shop there because it learned too late that China isn't a do-it-yourself market. Apparently, given how cheap labor is, middle-class Chinese consumers prefer to contract out their repairs. Imagining low demand in advance might have led to additional market research (asking Chinese consumers how they solve their home-repair problems) and a shift from do-it-yourself products to services.

Take an outside view

Now let's say you're in charge of a new-product development team. You've carefully devised a six-month plan—about which you are very confident—for initial design, consumer testing, and prototyping.

And you've carefully worked out what you'll need to manage the team optimally and why you expect to succeed. This is what Dan Lovallo and Daniel Kahneman call taking an "inside view" of the project, which typically results in excessive optimism. You need to complement this perspective with an outside view—one that considers what's happened with similar ventures and what advice you'd give someone else if you weren't involved in the endeavor. Analysis might show, for instance, that only 30% of new products in your industry have turned a profit within five years. Would you advise a colleague or a friend to accept a 70% chance of failure? If not, don't proceed unless you've got evidence that your chances of success are substantially better than everyone else's.

An outside view also prevents the "planning fallacy"—spinning a narrative of total success and managing for that, even though your odds of failure are actually pretty high. If you take a cold, hard look at the costs and the time required to develop new products in your market, you might see that they far outstrip your optimistic forecast, which in turn might lead you to change or scrap your plan.

Thinking About Objectives

It's important to have an expansive mindset about your objectives, too. This will help you focus when it's time to pick your most suitable options. Most people unwittingly limit themselves by allowing only a subset of worthy goals to guide them, simply because they're unaware of the full range of possibilities.

That's a trap the senior management team at Seagate Technology sought to avoid in the early 1990s, when the company was the world's largest manufacturer of disk drives. After acquiring a number of firms, Seagate approached the decision analyst Ralph Keeney for help in figuring out how to integrate them into a single organization. Keeney conducted individual interviews with 12 of Seagate's top executives, including the CEO, to elicit the firm's goals. By synthesizing their responses, he identified eight general objectives (such as creating the best software organization and providing value to customers) and 39 specific ones (such as developing better product standards and reducing customer costs). Tellingly, each executive named, on average, only about a third of the specific objectives, and only one person cited more than half. But with all the objectives mapped out, senior managers had a more comprehensive view and a shared framework for deciding which opportunities to pursue. If they hadn't systematically reflected on their goals, some of those prospects might have gone undetected.

Early in the decision-making process, you want to generate many objectives. Later you can sort out which ones matter most. Seagate, for example, placed a high priority on improving products because that would lead to more satisfied customers, more sales, and ultimately greater profits. Of course, there are other paths to greater profits, such as developing a leaner, more efficient workforce. Articulating, documenting, and organizing your goals helps you see those paths clearly so that you can choose the one that makes the most sense in light of probable outcomes.

Take these steps to ensure that you're reaching high—and far—enough with your objectives.

Seek advice

Round out your perspective by looking to others for ideas. In one study, researchers asked MBA students to list all their objectives for an internship. Most mentioned seven or eight things, such as "improve my attractiveness for full-time job offers" and "develop my leadership skills." Then they were shown a master list of everyone's objectives and asked which ones they considered personally relevant. Their own lists doubled in size as a result—and when participants ranked their goals afterward, those generated by others scored as high as those they had come up with themselves.

Outline objectives on your own before seeking advice so that you don't get "anchored" by what others say. And don't anchor your advisers by leading with what you already believe ("I think our new CFO needs to have experience with acquisitions—what do you think?"). If you are making a decision jointly with others, have people list their goals independently and then combine the lists, as Keeney did at Seagate.

Cycle through your objectives

Drawing on his consulting work and lab experiments, Keeney has found that looking at objectives one by one rather than all at once helps people come up with more alternatives. Seeking a solution that checks off every single box is too difficult—it paralyzes the decision maker.

So, when considering your goals for, say, an off-site retreat, tackle one at a time. If you want people to exchange lessons from the past year, develop certain leadership skills, and deepen their understanding of strategic priorities, thinking about these aims separately can help you achieve them more effectively. You might envision multiple sessions or even different events, from having expert facilitators lead brainstorming sessions to attending a leadership seminar at a top business school. Next, move on to combinations of objectives. To develop leadership skills and entertain accompanying family members, you might consider an Outward Bound–type experience. Even if you don't initially like an idea, write it down—it may spark additional ideas that satisfy even more objectives.

Thinking About Options

Although you need a critical mass of options to make sound decisions, you also need to find strong contenders—at least two but ideally three to five. Of course, it's easy to give in to the tug of System 1 thinking and generate a false choice to rationalize your intuitively favorite option (like a parent who asks an energetic toddler, "Would you like one nap or two today?"). But then you're just duping yourself. A decision can be no better than the best option under consideration. Even System 2 thinking is often too narrow. Analyzing the pros and cons of several options won't do you any good if you've failed to identify the best ones.

Unfortunately, people rarely consider more than one at a time. Managers tend to frame decisions as yes-or-no questions instead of generating alternatives. They might ask, for instance, "Should we expand our retail furniture business into Brazil?" without questioning whether expansion is even a good idea and whether Brazil is the best place to go.

Yes-no framing is just one way we narrow our options. Others include focusing on one type of solution to a problem (what psychologists call functional fixedness) and being constrained by our assumptions about what works and what doesn't. All these are signs of cognitive rigidity, which gets amplified when we feel threatened by time pressure, negative emotions, exhaustion, and other stressors. We devote mental energy to figuring out how to avoid a loss rather than developing new possibilities to explore.

Use joint evaluation

The problem with evaluating options in isolation is that you can't ensure the best outcomes. Take this scenario from a well-known study: A company is looking for a software engineer to write programs in a new computer language. There are two applicants, recent graduates of the same esteemed university. One has written 70 programs in the new language and has a 3.0 (out of 5.0) grade point average. The other has written 10 programs and has a 4.9 GPA. Who gets the higher offer?

The answer will probably depend on whether you look at both candidates side by side or just one. In the study, most people who considered the two programmers at the same time—in joint evaluation mode—wanted to pay more money to the more prolific recruit, despite his lower GPA. However, when other groups of people were asked about only one programmer each, proposed salaries were higher for the one with the better GPA. It is hard to know whether 70 programs is a lot or a little when you have no point of comparison. In separate evaluation mode, people pay attention to what they can easily evaluate—in this case, academic success—and ignore what they can't. They make a decision without considering all the relevant facts.

A proven way to snap into joint evaluation mode is to consider what you'll be missing if you make a certain choice. That forces you to search for other possibilities. In a study at Yale, 75% of respondents said yes when asked, "Would you buy a copy of an entertaining movie for $14.99?" But only 55% said yes when explicitly told they could either buy the movie or keep the money for other purchases. That simple shift to joint evaluation highlights what economists call the opportunity cost—what you give up when you pursue something else.

Try the "vanishing options" test

Once people have a solid option, they usually want to move on, so they fail to explore alternatives that may be superior. To address this problem, the decision experts Chip Heath and Dan Heath recommend a mental trick: Assume you can't choose any of the options you're weighing and ask, "What else could I do?" This question will trigger an exploration of alternatives. You could use it to open up your thinking about expanding your furniture business to Brazil: "What if we *couldn't* invest in South America? What else could we do with our resources?" That might prompt you to consider investing in another region instead, making improvements in your current location, or giving the online store a major upgrade. If more than one idea looked promising, you might split the difference: for instance, test the waters in Brazil by leasing stores instead of building them, and use the surplus for improvements at home.

Fighting Motivated Bias

All these cognitive biases—narrow thinking about the future, about objectives, and about options—are said to be "motivated" when driven by an intense psychological need, such as a strong emotional attachment or investment. Motivated biases are especially difficult to overcome. You know this if you've ever poured countless hours and resources into developing an idea, only to discover months later that someone has beaten you to it. You should move on, but your desire to avoid a loss is so great that it distorts your perception of benefits and risks. And so you feel an overwhelming urge to forge ahead—to prove that your idea is somehow bigger or better.

Our misguided faith in our own judgment makes matters worse. We're overconfident for two reasons: We give the information we do have too much weight (see the sidebar "How to Prevent Misweighting"). And because we don't know what we can't see, we have trouble imagining other ways of framing the problem or working toward a solution.

But we can preempt some motivated biases, such as the tendency to doggedly pursue a course of action we desperately want to take,

How to Prevent Misweighting

WHEN WE ASSIGN TOO MUCH or too little significance to the information we have, we're bound to go off course in our decision making. It's a problem that cuts across the different types of bias, but here are some tactics that can help.

	Examples
Blinding Improves judgment by eliminating the influence of stereotypes, idiosyncratic associations, and irrelevant factors.	Orchestras have players audition behind a screen to prevent gender bias. After this became standard practice, female membership skyrocketed from 5% in 1970 to nearly 40% today. Many professors ensure fair grading by covering up names (or asking an assistant to do so) before evaluating papers and other assignments.
Checklists Reduce errors due to forgetfulness and other memory distortions by directing our attention to what's most relevant.	Venture capitalists often use a set list of criteria to vet entrepreneurial pitches. Savvy hiring managers assess candidates by conducting structured interviews (they're much more accurate predictors of performance than open-ended interviews). Because there's a standard way to rate responses, people can be easily compared on various dimensions.
Algorithms Ensure consistency by predetermining how much emphasis each piece of information will get.*	Banks and other lenders use scoring algorithms to predict consumers' creditworthiness. Taking a page from professional baseball, employers are starting to use algorithms in hiring. One study showed that a simple equation for evaluating applicants outperformed human judgment by at least 25%.

*Since algorithms reflect the biases of the experts who build them, it's best to combine them with other debiasing tools.

by using a "trip wire" to redirect ourselves to a more logical path. That's what many expedition guides do when leading clients up Mount Everest: They announce a deadline in advance. If the group fails to reach the summit by then, it must head back to camp—and depending on weather conditions, it may have to give up on the expedition entirely. From a rational perspective, the months of training and preparation amount to sunk costs and should be disregarded. When removed from the situation, nearly everyone would agree that ignoring the turnaround time would put lives at stake and be too risky. However, loss aversion is a powerful psychological force. Without a trip wire, many climbers do push ahead, unwilling to give up their dream of conquering the mountain. Their tendency to act on emotion is even stronger because System 2 thinking is incapacitated by low oxygen levels at high altitudes. As they climb higher, they become less decision-ready—and in greater need of a trip wire.

In business, trip wires can make people less vulnerable to "present bias"—the tendency to focus on immediate preferences and ignore long-term aims and consequences. For instance, if you publicly say *when* you'll seek the coaching that your boss wants you to get (and that you've been putting off even though you know it's good for you), you'll be more apt to follow through. Make your trip wire precise (name a date) so that you'll find it harder to disregard later, and share it with people who will hold you accountable.

Another important use of trip wires is in competitive bidding situations, where the time and effort already invested in a negotiation may feel like a loss if no deal is reached. Executives often try to avoid that loss by escalating their commitment, overpaying by millions or even billions of dollars. The thing is, preferences often change over the course of a negotiation (for example, new information that comes to light may justify paying a higher price). So in this sort of situation, consider setting a *decision point*—a kind of trip wire that's less binding because it triggers thinking instead of a certain action. If the deal price escalates beyond your trigger value, take a break and reassess your objectives and options. Decision points provide greater flexibility than "hard" trip wires, but because they allow for multiple courses of action, they also increase your risk of making short-term, emotion-based decisions.

Although narrow thinking can plague us at any time, we're especially susceptible to it when faced with one-off decisions, because we can't learn from experience. So tactics that broaden our perspective on possible futures, objectives, and options are particularly valuable in these situations. Some tools, such as checklists and algorithms, can improve decision readiness by reducing the burden on our memory or attention; others, such as trip wires, ensure our focus on a critical event when it happens.

As a rule of thumb, it's good to anticipate three possible futures, establish three key objectives, and generate three viable options for each decision scenario. We can always do more, of course, but this general approach will keep us from feeling overwhelmed by endless possibilities—which can be every bit as debilitating as seeing too few.

Even the smartest people exhibit biases in their judgments and choices. It's foolhardy to think we can overcome them through sheer will. But we *can* anticipate and outsmart them by nudging ourselves in the right direction when it's time to make a call.

Originally published in May 2015. Reprint R1505D

The 3-D Printing Revolution

by Richard D'Aveni

INDUSTRIAL 3-D PRINTING is at a tipping point, about to go mainstream in a big way. Most executives and many engineers don't realize it, but this technology has moved well beyond prototyping, rapid tooling, trinkets, and toys. "Additive manufacturing" is creating durable and safe products for sale to real customers in moderate to large quantities.

The beginnings of the revolution show up in a 2014 PwC survey of more than 100 manufacturing companies. At the time of the survey, 11% had already switched to volume production of 3-D-printed parts or products. According to Gartner analysts, a technology is "mainstream" when it reaches an adoption level of 20%.

Among the numerous companies using 3-D printing to ramp up production are GE (jet engines, medical devices, and home appliance parts), Lockheed Martin and Boeing (aerospace and defense), Aurora Flight Sciences (unmanned aerial vehicles), Invisalign (dental devices), Google (consumer electronics), and the Dutch company LUXeXcel (lenses for light-emitting diodes, or LEDs). Watching these developments, McKinsey recently reported that 3-D printing is "ready to emerge from its niche status and become a viable alternative to conventional manufacturing processes in an increasing number of applications." In 2014 sales of industrial-grade 3-D printers in the United States were already one-third the volume of industrial automation and robotic sales. Some projections have that figure rising to 42% by 2020.

More companies will follow as the range of printable materials continues to expand. In addition to basic plastics and photosensitive resins, these already include ceramics, cement, glass, numerous metals and metal alloys, and new thermoplastic composites infused with carbon nanotubes and fibers. Superior economics will eventually convince the laggards. Although the direct costs of producing goods with these new methods and materials are often higher, the greater flexibility afforded by additive manufacturing means that total costs can be substantially lower.

With this revolutionary shift already under way, managers should now be engaging with strategic questions on three levels:

First, sellers of tangible products should ask how their *offerings* could be improved, whether by themselves or by competitors. Fabricating an object layer by layer, according to a digital "blueprint" downloaded to a printer, allows not only for limitless customization but also for designs of greater intricacy.

Second, industrial enterprises must revisit their *operations*. As additive manufacturing creates myriad new options for how, when, and where products and parts are fabricated, what network of supply chain assets and what mix of old and new processes will be optimal?

Third, leaders must consider the strategic implications as whole commercial *ecosystems* begin to form around the new realities of 3-D printing. Much has been made of the potential for large swaths of the manufacturing sector to atomize into an untold number of small "makers." But that vision tends to obscure a surer and more important development: To permit the integration of activities across designers, makers, and movers of goods, digital platforms will have to be established. At first these platforms will enable design-to-print activities and design sharing and fast downloading. Soon they will orchestrate printer operations, quality control, real-time optimization of printer networks, and capacity exchanges, among other needed functions. The most successful platform providers will prosper mightily by establishing standards and providing the settings in which a complex ecosystem can coordinate responses to market demands. But every

Idea in Brief

The Breakthrough

Additive manufacturing, or 3-D printing, is poised to transform the industrial economy. Its extreme flexibility not only allows for easy customization of goods but also eliminates assembly and inventories and enables products to be redesigned for higher performance.

The Challenge

Management teams should be reconsidering their strategies along three dimensions: (1) How might our offerings be enhanced, either by us or by competitors? (2) How should we reconfigure our operations, given the myriad new options for fabricating products and parts? (3) How will our commercial ecosystem evolve?

The Big Play

Inevitably, powerful platforms will arise to establish standards and facilitate exchanges among the designers, makers, and movers of 3-D-printed goods. The most successful of these will prosper mightily.

company will be affected by the rise of these platforms. There will be much jockeying among incumbents and upstarts to capture shares of the enormous value this new technology will create.

These questions add up to a substantial amount of strategic thinking, and still another remains: How fast will all this happen? For a given business, here's how fast it *can* happen: The U.S. hearing aid industry converted to 100% additive manufacturing in less than 500 days, according to one industry CEO, and not one company that stuck to traditional manufacturing methods survived. Managers will need to determine whether it's wise to wait for this fast-evolving technology to mature before making certain investments or whether the risk of waiting is too great. Their answers will differ, but for all of them it seems safe to say that the time for strategic thinking is now.

Additive's Advantages

It may be hard to imagine that this technology will displace today's standard ways of making things in large quantities. Traditional injection-molding presses, for example, can spit out thousands of widgets an hour. By contrast, people who have watched 3-D printers in action in the hobbyist market often find the layer-by-layer accretion of objects comically slow. But recent advances in the technology are changing that dramatically in industrial settings.

Some may forget why standard manufacturing occurs with such impressive speed. Those widgets pour out quickly because heavy investments have been made up front to establish the complex array of machine tools and equipment required to produce them. The first unit is extremely expensive to make, but as identical units follow, their marginal cost plummets.

Additive manufacturing doesn't offer anything like that economy of scale. However, it avoids the downside of standard manufacturing—a lack of flexibility. Because each unit is built independently, it can easily be modified to suit unique needs or, more broadly, to accommodate improvements or changing fashion. And setting up the production system in the first place is much simpler, because it involves far fewer stages. That's why 3-D printing has been so valuable for producing one-offs such as prototypes and rare replacement parts. But additive manufacturing increasingly makes sense even at higher scale. Buyers can choose from endless combinations of shapes, sizes, and colors, and this customization adds little to a manufacturer's cost even as orders reach mass-production levels.

A big part of the additive advantage is that pieces that used to be molded separately and then assembled can now be produced as one piece in a single run. A simple example is sunglasses: The 3-D process allows the porosity and mixture of plastics to vary in different areas of the frame. The earpieces come out soft and flexible, while the rims holding the lenses are hard. No assembly required.

Printing parts and products also allows them to be designed with more-complex architectures, such as honeycombing within steel panels or geometries previously too fine to mill. Complex mechanical parts—an encased set of gears, for example—can be made without assembly. Additive methods can be used to combine parts and generate far more interior detailing. That's why GE Aviation has switched to printing the fuel nozzles of certain jet engines. It expects to churn out more than 45,000 of the same design a year, so one might assume that conventional manufacturing methods would be more suitable. But printing technology allows a nozzle that used to be assembled from 20 separately cast parts to be fabricated in one piece. GE says this will cut the cost of manufacturing by 75%.

Additive manufacturing can also use multiple printer jets to lay down different materials simultaneously. Thus Optomec and other companies are developing conductive materials and methods of printing microbatteries and electronic circuits directly into or onto the surfaces of consumer electronic devices. Additional applications include medical equipment, transportation assets, aerospace components, measurement devices, telecom infrastructure, and many other "smart" things.

The enormous appeal of limiting assembly work is pushing additive manufacturing equipment to grow ever larger. At the current extreme, the U.S. Department of Defense, Lockheed Martin, Cincinnati Tool Steel, and Oak Ridge National Laboratory are partnering to develop a capability for printing most of the endo- and exoskeletons of jet fighters, including the body, wings, internal structural panels, embedded wiring and antennas, and soon the central load-bearing structure. So-called big area additive manufacturing makes such large-object fabrication possible by using a huge gantry with computerized controls to move the printers into position. When this process has been certified for use, the only assembly required will be the installation of plug-and-play electronics modules for navigation, communications, weaponry, and electronic countermeasure systems in bays created during the printing process. In Iraq and Afghanistan the U.S. military has been using drones from Aurora Flight Sciences, which prints the entire body of these unmanned aerial vehicles—some with wingspans of 132 feet—in one build.

Three-Dimensional Strategy

This brief discussion of additive manufacturing's advantages suggests how readily companies will embrace the technology—and additional savings in inventory, shipping, and facility costs will make the case even stronger. The clear implication is that managers in companies of all kinds should be working to anticipate how their businesses will adapt on the three strategic levels mentioned above.

Offerings, redesigned

Product strategy is the answer to that most basic question in business, What will we sell? Companies will need to imagine how their customers could be better served in an era of additive manufacturing. What designs and features will now be possible that were not before? What aspects can be improved because restrictions or delivery delays have been eliminated?

For example, in the aerospace and automotive industries, 3-D printing will most often be used in the pursuit of performance gains. Previously, the fuel efficiency of jet fighters and vehicles could be enhanced by reducing their weight, but this frequently made them less structurally sound. The new technology allows manufacturers to hollow out a part to make it lighter and more fuel-efficient and incorporate internal structures that provide greater tensile strength, durability, and resistance to impact. And new materials that have greater heat and chemical resistance can be used in various spots in a product, as needed.

In other industries, the use of additive manufacturing for more-tailored and fast-evolving products will have ramifications for how offerings are marketed. What happens to the concept of product generations—let alone the hoopla around a launch—when things can be upgraded continually during successive printings rather than in the quantum leaps required by the higher tooling costs and setup times of conventional manufacturing? Imagine a near future in which cloud-based artificial intelligence augments additive manufacturing's ability to change or add products instantly without retooling. Real-time changes in product strategy, such as product mix and design decisions, would become possible. With such rapid adaptation, what new advantages should be core to brand promises? And how could marketing departments prevent brand drift without losing sales?

Operations, reoptimized

Operations strategy encompasses all the questions of how a company will buy, make, move, and sell goods. The answers will be very different with additive manufacturing. Greater operational efficiency is always a goal, but it can be achieved in many ways. Today most companies contemplating the use of the technology do

The Tipping Point in Patents

WANT TO KNOW HOW fast the 3-D future is coming? Don't look only at adoption rates among manufacturers. Look at the innovation rates of inventors.

In 2005 only 80 patents relating to additive manufacturing materials, software, and equipment were granted worldwide, not counting duplicates filed in multiple countries. By 2013 that number had gone into orbit, with approximately 600 new nonduplicative patents issued around the globe.

What are some of the companies behind these patents? Not surprisingly, the two leaders are Stratasys and 3D Systems, rivals that have staked out positions in additive manufacturing. They hold 57 and 49 nonduplicative patents respectively. As befits its printing heritage, Xerox, too, has invested heavily in additive technologies for making electronics and has developed a strong alliance with 3D Systems. Panasonic, Hewlett-Packard, 3M, and Siemens likewise hold numerous patents.

But surprisingly, the largest *users* of 3-D printing have also been active innovators. Fourth on the list, with 35 patents, is Therics, a manufacturer of medical devices. These commercial companies understand additive manufacturing's potential to give them important advantages over competitors.

Also noteworthy among patent holders are companies that straddle both worlds. GE and IBM are important manufacturers but are increasingly invested in platforms that optimize value chains run by other companies. GE (11 patents) is developing the industrial internet, and IBM (19) has worked out what it is calling the "software-defined supply chain" and optimization software for smart manufacturing systems. Both are well positioned to take on similar roles with regard to additive manufacturing—and both bear watching as models for how incumbents can capture disproportionate value from a highly disruptive technology.

Additive manufacturing patents issued worldwide

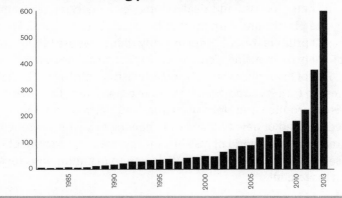

piecemeal financial analysis of targeted opportunities to swap in 3-D equipment and designs where those can reduce direct costs. Much bigger gains will come when they broaden their analyses to consider the total cost of manufacturing and overhead.

How much could be saved by cutting out assembly steps? Or by slashing inventories through production only in response to actual demand? Or by selling in different ways—for example, direct to consumers via interfaces that allow them to specify any configuration? In a hybrid world of old and new manufacturing methods, producers will have many more options; they will have to decide which components or products to transition over to additive manufacturing, and in what order.

Additional questions will arise around facilities locations. How proximate should they be to which customers? How can highly customized orders be delivered as efficiently as they are produced? Should printing be centralized in plants or dispersed in a network of printers at distributors, at retailers, on trucks, or even in customers' facilities? Perhaps all of the above. The answers will change in real time, adjusting to shifts in foreign exchange, labor costs, printer efficiency and capabilities, material costs, energy costs, and shipping costs.

A shorter traveling distance for products or parts not only saves money; it saves time. If you've ever been forced to leave your vehicle at a repair shop while the mechanic waits for a part, you'll appreciate that. BMW and Honda, among other automakers, are moving toward the additive manufacturing of many industrial tools and end-use car parts in their factories and dealerships—especially as new metal, composite plastic, and carbon-fiber materials become available for use in 3-D printers. Distributors in many industries are taking note, eager to help their business customers capitalize on the new efficiencies. UPS, for example, is building on its existing third-party logistics business to turn its airport hub warehouses into mini-factories. The idea is to produce and deliver customized parts to customers as needed, instead of devoting acres of shelving to vast inventories. If we already live in a world of just-in-time inventory management, we now see how JIT things can get. Welcome to instantaneous inventory management.

Indeed, given all the potential efficiencies of highly integrated additive manufacturing, business process management may become the most important capability around. Some companies that excel in this area will build out proprietary coordination systems to secure competitive advantage. Others will adopt and help to shape standard packages created by big software companies.

Ecosystems, reconfigured

Finally comes the question of where and how the enterprise fits into its broader business environment. Here managers address the puzzles of Who are we? and What do we need to own to be who we are? As additive manufacturing allows companies to acquire printers that can make many products, and as idle capacity is traded with others in the business of offering different products, the answers to those questions will become far less clear. Suppose you have rows of printers in your facility that build auto parts one day, military equipment the next day, and toys the next. What industry are you part of? Traditional boundaries will blur. Yet managers need a strong sense of the company's role in the world to make decisions about which assets they will invest in—or divest themselves of.

They may find their organizations evolving into something very different from what they have been. As companies are freed from many of the logistical requirements of standard manufacturing, they will have to look anew at the value of their capabilities and other assets and how those complement or compete with the capabilities of others.

The Platform Opportunity

One position in the ecosystem will prove to be the most central and powerful—and this fact is not lost on the management teams of the biggest players already in the business of additive manufacturing, such as eBay, IBM, Autodesk, PTC, Materialise, Stratasys, and 3D Systems. Many are vying to develop the platforms on which other companies will build and connect. They know that the role of platform provider is the biggest strategic objective they could pursue and that it's still very much up for grabs.

Three Ways to Wade into 3-D

ANY MANUFACTURER whose strategy for the future includes additive techniques has to lay out a road map for getting there. Companies already on the journey are taking things step-by-step, but in three different ways.

Trickle Down

Some start with their high-end products, knowing that their most sophisticated (and price-insensitive) customers will appreciate the innovation and flexibility. The luxury will trickle down in the time-honored way as the technology matures and becomes more affordable. Automotive manufacturers, for example, tend to engineer one-off parts specially for Formula One racing cars and then find ways to introduce versions of those innovations to high-end sports and luxury cars. As engineers' familiarity with the technology grows, they spot opportunities to bring it to parts for mass-market car segments.

Swap Out

Other pioneers proceed in a less splashy way, focusing first on the components of a given product that are easiest to migrate to additive manufacturing. The objective is to develop the organization's know-how by advancing to more-challenging components of the same product. This is common in aerospace, where companies have selected a specific product, such as an F-35 fighter jet, and started with mundane brackets and braces before moving to, say, internal panels and partitions. As the manufacturers learn more,

Platforms are a prominent feature in highly digitized 21st-century markets, and additive manufacturing will be no exception. Here platform owners will be powerful because production itself is likely to matter less over time. Already some companies are setting up contract "printer farms" that will effectively commoditize the making of products on demand. Even the valuable designs for printable products, being purely digital and easily shared, will be hard to hold tight. (For that matter, 3-D scanning devices will make it possible to reverse-engineer products by capturing their geometric design information.)

Everyone in the system will have a stake in sustaining the platforms on which production is dynamically orchestrated, blueprints are stored and continually enhanced, raw materials supplies are monitored and purchased, and customer orders are received. Those that control the digital ecosystem will sit in the middle of a they begin printing the fighter's exterior skin. Experiments with printing its load-bearing structures are now under way.

Cut Across

A third approach is to find components that show up in multiple products and use them to establish a 3-D foothold. For example, a design improvement for a fighter jet could be transferred to drones, missiles, or satellites. Such cross-product improvement builds knowledge and awareness throughout the company of how additive manufacturing can enhance performance on key dimensions such as weight, energy use, and flexibility.

The common theme here is small, incremental steps. In all three approaches, engineers are being given fascinating new puzzles to solve without having their world upended by still-evolving methods and materials, thus minimizing risk and resistance to change. It is up to more-senior managers to maintain the appropriate level of pressure for taking each successive step. As they push for further adoption, they should allow naysayers to explain why 3-D printing isn't right for a given part or process, but then challenge them to overcome that roadblock. Traditionalists will always be quick to tell you what 3-D printing can't do. Don't let them blind you to what it can.

tremendous volume of industrial transactions, collecting and selling valuable information. They will engage in arbitrage and divide the work up among trusted parties or assign it in-house when appropriate. They will trade printer capacity and designs all around the world, influencing prices by controlling or redirecting the "deal flow" for both. Like commodities arbitrageurs, they will finance trades or buy low and sell high with the asymmetric information they gain from overseeing millions of transactions.

Responsibility for aligning dispersed capacity with growing market demand will fall to a small number of companies—and if the whole system is to work efficiently, some will have to step up to it. Look for analogs to Google, eBay, Match.com, and Amazon to emerge as search engines, exchange platforms, branded market-places, and matchmakers among additive manufacturing printers, designers, and design repositories. Perhaps even automated trading will come into existence, along with markets for trading derivatives or futures on printer capacity and designs.

In essence, then, the owners of printer-based manufacturing assets will compete with the owners of information for the profits generated by the ecosystem. And in fairly short order, power will migrate from producers to large systems integrators, which will set up branded platforms with common standards to coordinate and support the system. They'll foster innovation through open sourcing and acquiring or partnering with smaller companies that meet high standards of quality. Small companies may indeed continue to try out interesting new approaches on the margins—but we'll need big organizations to oversee the experiments and then push them to be practical and scalable.

Digital History Replicated

Thinking about the unfolding revolution in additive manufacturing, it's hard not to reflect on that great transformative technology, the internet. In terms of the latter's history, it might be fair to say that additive manufacturing is only in 1995. Hype levels were high that year, yet no one imagined how commerce and life would change in the coming decade, with the arrival of Wi-Fi, smartphones, and cloud computing. Few foresaw the day that internet-based artificial intelligence and software systems could run factories—and even city infrastructures—better than people could.

The future of additive manufacturing will bring similar surprises that might look strictly logical in hindsight but are hard to picture today. Imagine how new, highly capable printers might replace highly skilled workers, shifting entire companies and even manufacturing-based countries into people-less production. In "machine organizations," humans might work only to service the printers.

And that future will arrive quickly. Once companies put a toe in the water and experience the advantages of greater manufacturing flexibility, they tend to dive in deep. As materials science creates more printable substances, more manufacturers and products will follow. Local Motors recently demonstrated that it can print a good-looking roadster, including wheels, chassis, body, roof, interior seats, and dashboard but not yet drivetrain, from bottom to top in 48 hours. When it goes into production, the roadster, including drivetrain, will be priced at approximately $20,000. As the cost of 3-D equipment and materials falls, traditional methods' remaining advantages in economies of scale are becoming a minor factor.

Here's what we can confidently expect: Within the next five years we will have fully automated, high-speed, large-quantity additive manufacturing systems that are economical even for standardized parts. Owing to the flexibility of those systems, customization or fragmentation in many product categories will then take off, further reducing conventional mass production's market share.

Smart business leaders aren't waiting for all the details and eventualities to reveal themselves. They can see clearly enough that additive manufacturing developments will change the way products are designed, made, bought, and delivered. They are taking the first steps in the redesign of manufacturing systems. They are envisioning the claims they will stake in the emerging ecosystem. They are making the many layers of decisions that will add up to advantage in a new world of 3-D printing.

Originally published in May 2015. Reprint R1505B

Why Strategy Execution Unravels—and What to Do About It

by Donald Sull, Rebecca Homkes, and Charles Sull

SINCE MICHAEL PORTER'S seminal work in the 1980s we have had a clear and widely accepted definition of what strategy is—but we know a lot less about translating a strategy into results. Books and articles on strategy outnumber those on execution by an order of magnitude. And what little has been written on execution tends to focus on tactics or generalize from a single case. So what do we know about strategy execution?

We know that it matters. A recent survey of more than 400 global CEOs found that executional excellence was the number one challenge facing corporate leaders in Asia, Europe, and the United States, heading a list of some 80 issues, including innovation, geopolitical instability, and top-line growth. We also know that execution is difficult. Studies have found that two-thirds to three-quarters of large organizations struggle to implement their strategies.

Nine years ago one of us (Don) began a large-scale project to understand how complex organizations can execute their strategies more effectively. The research includes more than 40 experiments in which we made changes in companies and measured the impact on execution, along with a survey administered to nearly 8,000 managers in more than 250 companies (see the sidebar "About the

Research"). The study is ongoing but has already produced valuable insights. The most important one is this: Several widely held beliefs about how to implement strategy are just plain wrong. In this article we debunk five of the most pernicious myths and replace them with a more accurate perspective that will help managers effectively execute strategy.

Myth 1: Execution Equals Alignment

Over the past few years we have asked managers from hundreds of companies, before they take our survey, to describe how strategy is executed in their firms. Their accounts paint a remarkably consistent picture. The steps typically consist of translating strategy into objectives, cascading those objectives down the hierarchy, measuring progress, and rewarding performance. When asked how they would improve execution, the executives cite tools, such as management by objectives and the balanced scorecard, that are designed to increase alignment between activities and strategy up and down the chain of command. In the managers' minds, execution equals alignment, so a failure to execute implies a breakdown in the processes to link strategy to action at every level in the organization.

Despite such perceptions, it turns out that in the vast majority of companies we have studied, those processes are sound. Research on strategic alignment began in the 1950s with Peter Drucker's work on management by objectives, and by now we know a lot about achieving alignment. Our research shows that best practices are well established in today's companies. More than 80% of managers say that their goals are limited in number, specific, and measurable and that they have the funds needed to achieve them. If most companies are doing everything right in terms of alignment, why are they struggling to execute their strategies?

To find out, we ask survey respondents how frequently they can count on others to deliver on promises—a reliable measure of whether things in an organization get done (see "Promise-Based Management: The Essence of Execution," by Donald N. Sull and Charles Spinosa, HBR, April 2007). Fully 84% of managers say they

Idea in Brief

The Problem

We have thousands of guides about developing a strategy—but very few about how to actually execute one. And the difficulty of achieving executional excellence is a major obstacle at most companies.

The Research

Executives attribute poor execution to a lack of alignment and a weak performance culture.

It turns out, though, that in most businesses activities line up well with strategic goals, and the people who meet their numbers are consistently rewarded.

The Recommendations

To execute their strategies, companies must foster coordination across units and build the agility to adapt to changing market conditions.

can rely on their boss and their direct reports all or most of the time—a finding that would make Drucker proud but sheds little light on why execution fails. When we ask about commitments across functions and business units, the answer becomes clear. Only 9% of managers say they can rely on colleagues in other functions and units all the time, and just half say they can rely on them most of the time. Commitments from these colleagues are typically not much more reliable than promises made by external partners, such as distributors and suppliers.

When managers cannot rely on colleagues in other functions and units, they compensate with a host of dysfunctional behaviors that undermine execution: They duplicate effort, let promises to customers slip, delay their deliverables, or pass up attractive opportunities. The failure to coordinate also leads to conflicts between functions and units, and these are handled badly two times out of three—resolved after a significant delay (38% of the time), resolved quickly but poorly (14%), or simply left to fester (12%).

Even though, as we've seen, managers typically equate execution with alignment, they do recognize the importance of coordination when questioned about it directly. When asked to identify the single greatest challenge to executing their company's strategy, 30% cite failure to coordinate across units, making that a close second to failure to align (40%). Managers also say they are three times more

About the Research

FIVE YEARS AGO we developed an in-depth survey that we have administered to 7,600 managers in 262 companies across 30 industries to date. We used the following principles in its design.

Focus on complex organizations in volatile markets. The companies in our sample are typically large (6,000 employees, on average, and median annual sales of $430 million) and compete in volatile sectors: Financial services, information technology, telecommunications, and oil and gas are among the most highly represented. One-third are based in emerging markets.

Target those in the know. We ask companies to identify the leaders most critical to driving execution, and we send the survey to those named. On average, 30 managers per company respond. They represent multiple organizational layers, including top team members (13%), their direct reports (28%), other middle managers (25%), frontline supervisors and team leaders (20%), and technical and domain experts and others (14%).

Gather objective data. Whenever possible, we structure questions to elicit objective information. For example, to assess how well executives communicate strategy, we ask respondents to list their companies' strategic priorities for the next few years; we then code the responses and test their convergence with one another and their consistency with management's stated objectives.

Engage the respondents. To prevent respondents from "checking out," we vary question formats and pose questions that managers view as important and have not been asked before. More than 95% of respondents finish the survey, spending an average of 40 minutes on it.

Link to credible research. Although the research on execution as a whole is not very advanced, some components of execution, such as goal setting, team dynamics, and resource allocation, are well understood. Whenever possible, we draw on research findings to design our questions and interpret our results.

---

likely to miss performance commitments because of insufficient support from other units than because of their own teams' failure to deliver.

Whereas companies have effective processes for cascading goals downward in the organization, their systems for managing horizontal performance commitments lack teeth. More than 80% of the companies we have studied have at least one formal system for managing commitments across silos, including cross-functional committees, service-level agreements, and centralized project-management offices—but only 20% of managers believe that these systems work well all or most of the time. More than half want more structure in the processes to coordinate activities across units—twice the number who want more structure in the management-by-objectives system.

Myth 2: Execution Means Sticking to the Plan

When crafting strategy, many executives create detailed road maps that specify who should do what, by when, and with what resources. The strategic-planning process has received more than its share of criticism, but, along with the budgeting process, it remains the backbone of execution in many organizations. Bain & Company, which regularly surveys large corporations around the world about their use of management tools, finds that strategic planning consistently heads the list. After investing enormous amounts of time and energy formulating a plan and its associated budget, executives view deviations as a lack of discipline that undercuts execution.

Unfortunately, no Gantt chart survives contact with reality. No plan can anticipate every event that might help or hinder a company trying to achieve its strategic objectives. Managers and employees at every level need to adapt to facts on the ground, surmount unexpected obstacles, and take advantage of fleeting opportunities. Strategy execution, as we define the term, consists of seizing opportunities that support the strategy while coordinating with other parts of the organization on an ongoing basis. When managers come up with creative solutions to unforeseen problems or run with unexpected opportunities, they are not undermining systematic implementation; they are demonstrating execution at its best.

Such real-time adjustments require firms to be agile. Yet a lack of agility is a major obstacle to effective execution among the companies we have studied. When asked to name the greatest challenge their companies will face in executing strategy over the next few years, nearly one-third of managers cite difficulties adapting to changing market circumstances. It's not that companies fail to adapt at all: Only one manager in 10 saw that as the problem.

Where Execution Breaks Down

OVER THE PAST FIVE YEARS the authors have surveyed nearly 8,000 managers in more than 250 companies about strategy execution. The responses paint a remarkably consistent picture.

We can rely on people in the chain of command, suggesting that alignment up and down the hierarchy is not a problem.

Share of managers who say they can rely all or most of the time on:

Their boss

84%

Their direct reports

84%

But coordination is a problem: People in other units are not much more reliable than external partners are.

Share who say they can rely all or most of the time on:

Colleagues in other departments

59%

External partners

56%

But most organizations either react so slowly that they can't seize fleeting opportunities or mitigate emerging threats (29%), or react quickly but lose sight of company strategy (24%). Just as managers want more structure in the processes to support coordination, they crave more structure in the processes used to adapt to changing circumstances.

A seemingly easy solution would be to do a better job of resource allocation. Although resource allocation is unquestionably critical to execution, the term itself is misleading. In volatile markets, the allotment of funds, people, and managerial attention is not a onetime decision; it requires ongoing adjustment. According to a study by McKinsey, firms that actively *reallocated* capital expenditures across business units achieved an average shareholder return

We don't adapt quickly enough to changing market conditions.

Share who say their organizations effectively:

Shift funds across units to support strategy

30%

Shift people across units to support strategy

20%

Exit declining businesses/unsuccessful initiatives

22%

And we invest in too many nonstrategic projects.

Share who say:

They could secure resources to pursue attractive opportunities outside their strategic objectives

51%

All their company's strategic priorities have the resources they need for success

11%

30% higher than the average return of companies that were slow to shift funds.

Instead of focusing on resource allocation, with its connotation of one-off choices, managers should concentrate on the fluid real-location of funds, people, and attention. We have noticed a pattern among the companies in our sample: Resources are often trapped in unproductive uses. Fewer than one-third of managers believe that their organizations reallocate funds to the right places quickly enough to be effective. The reallocation of people is even worse. Only 20% of managers say their organizations do a good job of shifting people across units to support strategic priorities. The rest report that their companies rarely shift people across units (47%) or else make shifts in ways that disrupt other units (33%).

Companies also struggle to disinvest. Eight in 10 managers say their companies fail to exit declining businesses or to kill unsuccessful initiatives quickly enough. Failure to exit undermines execution in an obvious way, by wasting resources that could be redeployed. Slow exits impede execution in more-insidious ways as well: Top executives devote a disproportionate amount of time and attention to businesses with limited upside and send in talented managers who often burn themselves out trying to save businesses that should have been shut down or sold years earlier. The longer top executives drag their feet, the more likely they are to lose the confidence of their middle managers, whose ongoing support is critical for execution.

A word of warning: Managers should not invoke agility as an excuse to chase every opportunity that crosses their path. Many companies in our sample lack strategic discipline when deciding which new opportunities to pursue. Half the middle managers we have surveyed believe that they could secure significant resources to pursue attractive opportunities that fall *outside* their strategic objectives. This may sound like good news for any individual manager, but it spells trouble for a company as a whole, leading to the pursuit of more initiatives than resources can support. Only 11% of the managers we have surveyed believe that all their company's strategic priorities have the financial and human resources needed for success. That's a shocking statistic: It means that nine managers in 10 expect some of their organizations' major initiatives to fail for lack of resources. Unless managers screen opportunities against company strategy, they will waste time and effort on peripheral initiatives and deprive the most promising ones of the resources they need to win big. Agility is critical to execution, but it must fit within strategic boundaries. In other words, agility must be balanced with alignment.

Myth 3: Communication Equals Understanding

Many executives believe that relentlessly communicating strategy is a key to success. The CEO of one London-based professional services firm met with her management team the first week of every month and began each meeting by reciting the firm's strategy and its key priorities for the year. She was delighted when an employee engagement survey (not ours) revealed that 84% of all staff members agreed with the statement "I am clear on our organization's top priorities." Her efforts seemed to be paying off.

Then her management team took our survey, which asks members to describe the firm's strategy in their own words and to list the top five strategic priorities. Fewer than one-third could name even two. The CEO was dismayed—after all, she discussed those objectives in every management meeting. Unfortunately, she is not alone. Only 55% of the middle managers we have surveyed can name even one of their company's top five priorities. In other words, when the leaders charged with explaining strategy to the troops are given five chances to list their company's strategic objectives, nearly half fail to get even one right.

Not only are strategic objectives poorly understood, but they often seem unrelated to one another and disconnected from the overall strategy. Just over half of all top team members say they have a clear sense of how major priorities and initiatives fit together. It's pretty dire when half the C-suite cannot connect the dots between strategic priorities, but matters are even worse elsewhere. Fewer than one-third of senior executives' direct reports clearly understand the connections between corporate priorities, and the share plummets to 16% for frontline supervisors and team leaders.

Senior executives are often shocked to see how poorly their company's strategy is understood throughout the organization. In their view, they invest huge amounts of time communicating strategy, in an unending stream of e-mails, management meetings, and town hall discussions. But the amount of communication is not the issue: Nearly 90% of middle managers believe that top leaders communicate the strategy frequently enough. How can so much communication yield so little understanding?

Part of the problem is that executives measure communication in terms of inputs (the number of e-mails sent or town halls hosted) rather than by the only metric that actually counts—how well key leaders understand what's communicated. A related problem occurs when executives dilute their core messages with peripheral consid-erations. The executives at one tech company, for example, went to great pains to present their company's strategy and objectives at the annual executive off-site. But they also introduced 11 corporate pri-orities (which were different from the strategic objectives), a list of core competencies (including one with nine templates), a set of cor-porate values, and a dictionary of 21 new strategic terms to be mas-tered. Not surprisingly, the assembled managers were baffled about what mattered most. When asked about obstacles to understanding the strategy, middle managers are four times more likely to cite a large number of corporate priorities and strategic initiatives than to mention a lack of clarity in communication. Top executives add to the confusion when they change their messages frequently—a prob-lem flagged by nearly one-quarter of middle managers.

Myth 4: A Performance Culture Drives Execution

When their companies fail to translate strategy into results, many executives point to a weak performance culture as the root cause. The data tells a different story. It's true that in most companies, the official culture—the core values posted on the company website, say—does not support execution. However, a company's true values reveal themselves when managers make hard choices—and here we have found that a focus on performance *does* shape behavior on a day-to-day basis.

Few choices are tougher than personnel decisions. When we ask about factors that influence who gets hired, praised, promoted, and fired, we see that most companies do a good job of recognizing and rewarding performance. Past performance is by far the most fre-quently named factor in promotion decisions, cited by two-thirds of all managers. Although harder to assess when bringing in new employees, it ranks among the top three influences on who gets hired. One-third of managers believe that performance is also recognized all or most of the time with nonfinancial rewards, such as private praise, public acknowledgment, and access to training opportuni-ties. To be sure, there is room for improvement, particularly when it comes to dealing with underperformers: A majority of the companies we have studied delay action (33%), address underperformance inconsistently (34%), or tolerate poor performance (11%). Overall, though, the companies in our sample have robust performance cultures—and yet they struggle to execute strategy. Why?

The answer is that a culture that supports execution must recognize and reward other things as well, such as agility, teamwork, and ambition. Many companies fall short in this respect. When making hiring or promotion decisions, for example, they place much less value on a manager's ability to adapt to changing circumstances—an indication of the agility needed to execute strategy—than on whether she has hit her numbers in the past. Agility requires a willingness to experiment, and many managers avoid experimentation because they fear the consequences of failure. Half the managers we have surveyed believe that their careers would suffer if they pursued but failed at novel opportunities or innovations. Trying new things inevitably entails setbacks, and honestly discussing the challenges involved increases the odds of long-term success. But corporate cultures rarely support the candid discussions necessary for agility. Fewer than one-third of managers say they can have open and honest discussions about the most difficult issues, while one-third say that many important issues are considered taboo.

An excessive emphasis on performance can impair execution in another subtle but important way. If managers believe that hitting their numbers trumps all else, they tend to make conservative performance commitments. When asked what advice they would give to a new colleague, two-thirds say they would recommend making commitments that the colleague could be sure to meet; fewer than one-third would recommend stretching for ambitious goals. This tendency to play it safe may lead managers to favor surefire cost reductions over risky growth, for instance, or to milk an existing business rather than experiment with a new business model.

The most pressing problem with many corporate cultures, however, is that they fail to foster the coordination that, as we've discussed, is essential to execution. Companies consistently get this wrong. When it comes to hires, promotions, and nonfinancial recognition, past performance is two or three times more likely than a track record of collaboration to be rewarded. Performance is critical, of course, but if it comes at the expense of coordination, it can undermine execution. We ask respondents what would happen to a manager in their organization who achieved his objectives but failed to collaborate with colleagues in other units. Only 20% believe the behavior would be addressed promptly; 60% believe it would be addressed inconsistently or after a delay, and 20% believe it would be tolerated.

Myth 5: Execution Should Be Driven from the Top

In his best-selling book *Execution,* Larry Bossidy describes how, as the CEO of AlliedSignal, he personally negotiated performance objectives with managers several levels below him and monitored their progress. Accounts like this reinforce the common image of a heroic CEO perched atop the org chart, driving execution. That approach can work—for a while. AlliedSignal's stock outperformed the market under Bossidy's leadership. However, as Bossidy writes, shortly after he retired "the discipline of execution...unraveled," and the company gave up its gains relative to the S&P 500.

Top-down execution has drawbacks in addition to the risk of unraveling after the departure of a strong CEO. To understand why, it helps to remember that effective execution in large, complex organizations emerges from countless decisions and actions at all levels. Many of those involve hard trade-offs: For example, synching up with colleagues in another unit can slow down a team that's trying to seize a fleeting opportunity, and screening customer requests against strategy often means turning away lucrative business. The leaders who are closest to the situation and can respond most quickly are best positioned to make the tough calls.

Concentrating power at the top may boost performance in the short term, but it degrades an organization's capacity to execute over the long run. Frequent and direct intervention from on high encourages middle managers to escalate conflicts rather than resolve them, and over time they lose the ability to work things out with colleagues in other units. Moreover, if top executives insist on making the important calls themselves, they diminish middle managers' decision-making skills, initiative, and ownership of results.

In large, complex organizations, execution lives and dies with a group we call "distributed leaders," which includes not only middle managers who run critical businesses and functions but also technical and domain experts who occupy key spots in the informal networks that get things done. The vast majority of these leaders try to do the right thing. Eight out of 10 in our sample say they are committed to doing their best to execute the strategy, even when they would like more clarity on what the strategy is.

Distributed leaders, not senior executives, represent "management" to most employees, partners, and customers. Their day-to-day actions, particularly how they handle difficult decisions and what behaviors they tolerate, go a long way toward supporting or undermining the corporate culture. In this regard, most distributed leaders shine. As assessed by their direct reports, more than 90% of middle managers live up to the organization's values all or most of the time. They do an especially good job of reinforcing performance, with nearly nine in 10 consistently holding team members accountable for results.

But although execution should be driven from the middle, it needs to be guided from the top. And our data suggests that many top executive teams could provide much more support. Distributed leaders are hamstrung in their efforts to translate overall company strategy into terms meaningful for their teams or units when top executives fail to ensure that they clearly understand that strategy. And as we've seen, such failure is not the exception but the rule.

Conflicts inevitably arise in any organization where different units pursue their own objectives. Distributed leaders are asked to shoulder much of the burden of working across silos, and many appear to be buckling under the load. A minority of middle managers consistently anticipate and avoid problems (15%) or resolve conflicts quickly and well (26%). Most resolve issues only after a significant delay (37%), try but fail to resolve them (10%), or don't address them at all (12%). Top executives could help by adding structured processes to facilitate coordination. In many cases they could also do a better job of modeling teamwork. One-third of distributed leaders believe that factions exist within the C-suite and that executives there focus on their own agendas rather than on what is best for the company.

Many executives try to solve the problem of execution by reducing it to a single dimension. They focus on tightening alignment up and down the chain of command—by improving existing processes, such as strategic planning and performance management, or adopting new tools, such as the balanced scorecard. These are useful measures, to be sure, but relying on them as the sole means of driving execution ignores the need for coordination and agility in volatile markets. If managers focus too narrowly on improving alignment, they risk developing ever more refined answers to the wrong question.

In the worst cases, companies slip into a dynamic we call the alignment trap. When execution stalls, managers respond by tightening the screws on alignment—tracking more performance metrics, for example, or demanding more-frequent meetings to monitor progress and recommend what to do. This kind of top-down scrutiny often deteriorates into micromanagement, which stifles the experimentation required for agility and the peer-to-peer interactions that drive coordination. Seeing execution suffer but not knowing why, managers turn once more to the tool they know best and further tighten alignment. The end result: Companies are trapped in a downward spiral in which more alignment leads to worse results.

If common beliefs about execution are incomplete at best and dangerous at worst, what should take their place? The starting point is a fundamental redefinition of execution as the ability to seize opportunities aligned with strategy while coordinating with other parts of the organization on an ongoing basis. Reframing execution in those terms can help managers pinpoint why it is stalling. Armed with a more comprehensive understanding, they can avoid pitfalls such as the alignment trap and focus on the factors that matter most for translating strategy into results.

Originally published in March 2015. Reprint R1503C

The Authenticity Paradox

by Herminia Ibarra

AUTHENTICITY HAS BECOME THE GOLD STANDARD for leadership. But a simplistic understanding of what it means can hinder your growth and limit your impact.

Consider Cynthia, a general manager in a health care organization. Her promotion into that role increased her direct reports 10-fold and expanded the range of businesses she oversaw—and she felt a little shaky about making such a big leap. A strong believer in transparent, collaborative leadership, she bared her soul to her new employees: "I want to do this job," she said, "but it's scary, and I need your help." Her candor backfired; she lost credibility with people who wanted and needed a confident leader to take charge.

Or take George, a Malaysian executive in an auto parts company where people valued a clear chain of command and made decisions by consensus. When a Dutch multinational with a matrix structure acquired the company, George found himself working with peers who saw decision making as a freewheeling contest for the best-debated ideas. That style didn't come easily to him, and it contradicted everything he had learned about humility growing up in his country. In a 360-degree debrief, his boss told him that he needed to sell his ideas and accomplishments more aggressively. George felt he had to choose between being a failure and being a fake.

Because going against our natural inclinations can make us feel like impostors, we tend to latch on to authenticity as an excuse for sticking with what's comfortable. But few jobs allow us to do that for long. That's doubly true when we advance in our careers or when demands or expectations change, as Cynthia, George, and countless other executives have discovered.

In my research on leadership transitions, I have observed that career advances require all of us to move way beyond our comfort zones. At the same time, however, they trigger a strong countervailing impulse to protect our identities: When we are unsure of ourselves or our ability to perform well or measure up in a new setting, we often retreat to familiar behaviors and styles.

But my research also demonstrates that the moments that most challenge our sense of self are the ones that can teach us the most about leading effectively. By viewing ourselves as works in progress and evolving our professional identities through trial and error, we can develop a personal style that feels right to us and suits our organizations' changing needs.

That takes courage, because learning, by definition, starts with unnatural and often superficial behaviors that can make us feel calculating instead of genuine and spontaneous. But the only way to avoid being pigeonholed and ultimately become better leaders is to do the things that a rigidly authentic sense of self would keep us from doing.

Why Leaders Struggle with Authenticity

The word "authentic" traditionally referred to any work of art that is an original, not a copy. When used to describe leadership, of course, it has other meanings—and they can be problematic. For example, the notion of adhering to one "true self" flies in the face of much research on how people evolve with experience, discovering facets of themselves they would never have unearthed through introspection alone. And being utterly transparent—disclosing every single thought and feeling—is both unrealistic and risky.

Idea in Brief

The Problem

When we view authenticity as an unwavering sense of self, we struggle to take on new challenges and bigger roles. The reality is that people learn—and change—who they are through experience.

The Solution

By trying out different leadership styles and behaviors, we grow more than we would through introspection alone. Experimenting with our identities allows us to find the right approach for ourselves and our organizations.

The Sticking Point

This adaptive approach to authenticity can make us feel like impostors, because it involves doing things that may not come naturally. But it's outside our comfort zones that we learn the most about leading effectively.

Leaders today struggle with authenticity for several reasons. First, we make more-frequent and more-radical changes in the kinds of work we do. As we strive to *improve* our game, a clear and firm sense of self is a compass that helps us navigate choices and progress toward our goals. But when we're looking to *change* our game, a too rigid self-concept becomes an anchor that keeps us from sailing forth, as it did at first with Cynthia.

Second, in global business, many of us work with people who don't share our cultural norms and have different expectations for how we should behave. It can often seem as if we have to choose between what is expected—and therefore effective—and what feels authentic. George is a case in point.

Third, identities are always on display in today's world of ubiquitous connectivity and social media. How we present ourselves—not just as executives but as people, with quirks and broader interests—has become an important aspect of leadership. Having to carefully curate a persona that's out there for all to see can clash with our private sense of self.

In dozens of interviews with talented executives facing new expectations, I have found that they most often grapple with authenticity in the following situations.

Taking charge in an unfamiliar role

As everyone knows, the first 90 days are critical in a new leadership role. First impressions form quickly, and they matter. Depending on their personalities, leaders respond very differently to the increased visibility and performance pressure.

Psychologist Mark Snyder, of the University of Minnesota, identified two psychological profiles that inform how leaders develop their personal styles. "High self-monitors"—or chameleons, as I call them—are naturally able and willing to adapt to the demands of a situation without feeling fake. Chameleons care about managing their public image and often mask their vulnerability with bluster. They may not always get it right the first time, but they keep trying on different styles like new clothes until they find a good fit for themselves and their circumstances. Because of that flexibility, they often advance rapidly. But chameleons can run into problems when people perceive them as disingenuous or lacking a moral center—even though they're expressing their "true" chameleon nature.

By contrast, "true-to-selfers" (Snyder's "low self-monitors") tend to express what they really think and feel, even when it runs counter to situational demands. The danger with true-to-selfers like Cynthia and George is that they may stick too long with comfortable behavior that prevents them from meeting new requirements, instead of evolving their style as they gain insight and experience.

Cynthia (whom I interviewed after her story appeared in a *Wall Street Journal* article by Carol Hymowitz) hemmed herself in like this. She thought she was setting herself up for success by staying true to her highly personal, full-disclosure style of management. She asked her new team for support, openly acknowledging that she felt a bit at sea. As she scrambled to learn unfamiliar aspects of the business, she worked tirelessly to contribute to every decision and solve every problem. After a few months, she was on the verge of burnout. To make matters worse, sharing her vulnerability with her team members so early on had damaged her standing. Reflecting on her transition some years later, Cynthia told me: "Being authentic doesn't mean that you can be held up to the light and people can see right through you." But at the time, that was how she saw it—and instead of building trust, she made people question her ability to do the job.

Delegating and communicating appropriately are only part of the problem in a case like this. A deeper-seated issue is finding the right mix of distance and closeness in an unfamiliar situation. Stanford psychologist Deborah Gruenfeld describes this as managing the tension between authority and approachability. To be authoritative, you privilege your knowledge, experience, and expertise over the team's, maintaining a measure of distance. To be approachable, you emphasize your relationships with people, their input, and their perspective, and you lead with empathy and warmth. Getting the balance right presents an acute authenticity crisis for true-to-selfers, who typically have a strong preference for behaving one way or the other. Cynthia made herself too approachable and vulnerable, and it undermined and drained her. In her bigger role, she needed more distance from her employees to gain their confidence and get the job done.

Selling your ideas (and yourself)

Leadership growth usually involves a shift from having good ideas to pitching them to diverse stakeholders. Inexperienced leaders, especially true-to-selfers, often find the process of getting buy-in distasteful because it feels artificial and political; they believe that their work should stand on its own merits.

Here's an example: Anne, a senior manager at a transportation company, had doubled revenue and fundamentally redesigned core processes in her unit. Despite her obvious accomplishments, however, her boss didn't consider her an inspirational leader. Anne also knew she was not communicating effectively in her role as a board member of the parent company. The chairman, a broad-brush thinker, often became impatient with her detail orientation. His feedback to her was "step up, do the vision thing." But to Anne that seemed like valuing form over substance. "For me, it is manipulation," she told me in an interview. "I can do the storytelling too, but I refuse to play on people's emotions. If the string-pulling is too obvious, I can't make myself do it." Like many aspiring leaders, she resisted crafting emotional messages to influence and inspire others because that felt less authentic to her than relying on facts, figures, and spreadsheets. As a result, she worked at cross-purposes with the board chairman, pushing hard on the facts instead of pulling him in as a valued ally.

Many managers know deep down that their good ideas and strong potential will go unnoticed if they don't do a better job of selling themselves. Still, they can't bring themselves to do it. "I try to build a network based on professionalism and what I can deliver for the business, not who I know," one manager told me. "Maybe that's not smart from a career point of view. But I can't go against my beliefs.... So I have been more limited in 'networking up.'"

Until we see career advancement as a way of extending our reach and increasing our impact in the organization—a collective win, not just a selfish pursuit—we have trouble feeling authentic when touting our strengths to influential people. True-to-selfers find it particularly hard to sell themselves to senior management when they most need to do so: when they are still unproven. Research shows, however, that this hesitancy disappears as people gain experience and become more certain of the value they bring.

Processing negative feedback

Many successful executives encounter serious negative feedback for the first time in their careers when they take on larger roles or responsibilities. Even when the criticisms aren't exactly new, they loom larger because the stakes are higher. But leaders often convince themselves that dysfunctional aspects of their "natural" style are the inevitable price of being effective.

Let's look at Jacob, a food company production manager whose direct reports gave him low marks in a 360 review on emotional intelligence, team building, and empowering others. One team member wrote that it was hard for Jacob to accept criticism. Another remarked that after an angry outburst, he'd suddenly make a joke as if nothing had happened, not realizing the destabilizing effect of his mood changes on those around him. For someone who genuinely believed that he'd built trust among his people, all this was tough to swallow.

Why Companies Are Pushing Authenticity Training

MANAGERS CAN CHOOSE from countless books, articles, and executive workshops for advice on how to be more authentic at work. Two trends help explain the exploding popularity of the concept and the training industry it has fed.

First, trust in business leaders fell to an all-time low in 2012, according to the Edelman Trust Barometer. Even in 2013, when trust began to climb back up, only 18% of people reported that they trusted business leaders to tell the truth, and fewer than half trusted businesses to do the right thing.

Second, employee engagement is at a nadir. A 2013 Gallup poll found that only 13% of employees worldwide are engaged at work. Only one in eight workers—out of roughly 180 million employees studied—is psychologically committed to his or her job. In study after study, frustration, burnout, disillusionment, and misalignment with personal values are cited among the biggest reasons for career change.

At a time when public confidence and employee morale are so low, it's no surprise that companies are encouraging leaders to discover their "true" selves.

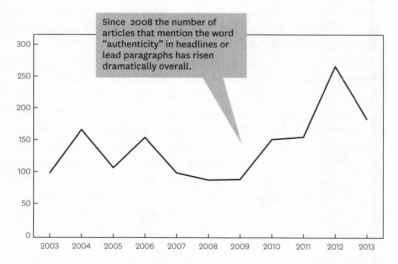

Since 2008 the number of articles that mention the word "authenticity" in headlines or lead paragraphs has risen dramatically overall.

Source: New York Times, Financial Times, Washington Post, Economist, Forbes, Wall Street Journal, and HBR

Once the initial shock had subsided, Jacob acknowledged that this was not the first time he'd received such criticism (some colleagues and subordinates had made similar comments a few years earlier). "I thought I'd changed my approach," he reflected, "but I haven't really changed so much since the last time." However, he quickly rationalized his behavior to his boss: "Sometimes you have to be tough in order to deliver results, and people don't like it," he said. "You have to accept that as part of the job description." Of course, he was missing the point.

Because negative feedback given to leaders often centers on style rather than skills or expertise, it can feel like a threat to their identity—as if they're being asked to give up their "secret sauce." That's how Jacob saw it. Yes, he could be explosive—but from his point of view, his "toughness" allowed him to deliver results year after year. In reality, though, he had succeeded up to this point *despite* his behavior. When his role expanded and he took on greater responsibility, his intense scrutiny of subordinates became an even bigger obstacle because it took up time he should have been devoting to more-strategic pursuits.

A great public example of this phenomenon is Margaret Thatcher. Those who worked with her knew she could be merciless if someone failed to prepare as thoroughly as she did. She was capable of humiliating a staff member in public, she was a notoriously bad listener, and she believed that compromise was cowardice. As she became known to the world as the "Iron Lady," Thatcher grew more and more convinced of the rightness of her ideas and the necessity of her coercive methods. She could beat anyone into submission with the power of her rhetoric and conviction, and she only got better at it. Eventually, though, it was her undoing—she was ousted by her own cabinet.

A Playful Frame of Mind

Such a rigid self-concept can result from too much introspection. When we look only within for answers, we inadvertently reinforce old ways of seeing the world and outdated views of ourselves.

Without the benefit of what I call outsight—the valuable external perspective we get from experimenting with new leadership behaviors—habitual patterns of thought and action fence us in. To begin thinking like leaders, we must first act: plunge ourselves into new projects and activities, interact with very different kinds of people, and experiment with new ways of getting things done. Especially in times of transition and uncertainty, thinking and introspection should follow experience—not vice versa. Action changes who we are and what we believe is worth doing.

Fortunately, there are ways of increasing outsight and evolving toward an "adaptively authentic" way of leading, but they require a playful frame of mind. Think of leadership development as trying on possible selves rather than working on yourself—which, let's face it, sounds like drudgery. When we adopt a playful attitude, we're more open to possibilities. It's OK to be inconsistent from one day to the next. That's not being a fake; it's how we experiment to figure out what's right for the new challenges and circumstances we face.

My research suggests three important ways to get started.

Learn from diverse role models

Most learning necessarily involves some form of imitation—and the understanding that nothing is "original." An important part of growing as a leader is viewing authenticity not as an intrinsic state but as the ability to take elements you have learned from others' styles and behaviors and make them your own.

But don't copy just one person's leadership style; tap many diverse role models. There is a big difference between imitating someone wholesale and borrowing selectively from various people to create your own collage, which you then modify and improve. As the playwright Wilson Mizner said, copying one author is plagiarism, but copying many is research.

I observed the importance of this approach in a study of investment bankers and consultants who were advancing from analytical and project work to roles advising clients and selling new business. Though most of them felt incompetent and insecure in their new positions, the chameleons among them consciously borrowed styles and tactics from successful senior leaders—learning through emulation how to use humor to break tension in meetings, for instance, and how to shape opinion without being overbearing. Essentially, the chameleons faked it until they found what worked for them. Noticing their efforts, their managers provided coaching and mentoring and shared tacit knowledge.

As a result, the chameleons arrived much faster at an authentic but more skillful style than the true-to-selfers in the study, who continued to focus solely on demonstrating technical mastery. Often the true-to-selfers concluded that their managers were "all talk and little content" and therefore not suitable role models. In the absence of a "perfect" model they had a harder time with imitation—it felt bogus. Unfortunately, their managers perceived their inability to adapt as a lack of effort or investment and thus didn't give them as much mentoring and coaching as they gave the chameleons.

Work on getting better

Setting goals for learning (not just for performance) helps us experiment with our identities without feeling like impostors, because we don't expect to get everything right from the start. We stop trying to protect our comfortable old selves from the threats that change can bring, and start exploring what kinds of leaders we might become.

Of course, we all want to perform well in a new situation—get the right strategy in place, execute like crazy, deliver results the organization cares about. But focusing exclusively on those things makes us afraid to take risks in the service of learning. In a series of ingenious experiments, Stanford psychologist Carol Dweck has shown that concern about how we will appear to others inhibits learning on new or unfamiliar tasks. Performance goals motivate us to show others that we possess valued attributes, such as intelligence and social skill, and to prove to ourselves that we have them. By contrast, learning goals motivate us to develop valued attributes.

When we're in performance mode, leadership is about presenting ourselves in the most favorable light. In learning mode, we can reconcile our yearning for authenticity in how we work and lead with an equally powerful desire to grow. One leader I met was highly

The Cultural Factor

WHATEVER THE SITUATION—taking charge in unfamiliar territory, selling your ideas and yourself, or processing negative feedback—finding authentic ways of being effective is even more difficult in a multicultural environment.

As my INSEAD colleague Erin Meyer finds in her research, styles of persuading others and the kinds of arguments that people find persuasive are far from universal; they are deeply rooted in a culture's philosophical, religious, and educational assumptions. That said, prescriptions for how leaders are supposed to look and sound are rarely as diverse as the leaders themselves. And despite corporate initiatives to build understanding of cultural differences and promote diversity, the fact is that leaders are still expected to express ideas assertively, to claim credit for them, and to use charisma to motivate and inspire people.

Authenticity is supposed to be an antidote to a single model of leadership. (After all, the message is to be yourself, not what someone else expects you to be.) But as the notion has gained currency, it has, ironically, come to mean something much more limiting and culturally specific. A closer look at how leaders are taught to discover and demonstrate authenticity—by telling a personal story about a hardship they have overcome, for example—reveals a model that is, in fact, very American, based on ideals such as self-disclosure, humility, and individualistic triumph over adversity.

This amounts to a catch-22 for managers from cultures with different norms for authority, communication, and collective endeavor because they must behave inauthentically in order to conform to the strictures of "authentic" leadership.

---

effective in small-group settings but struggled to convey openness to new ideas in larger meetings, where he often stuck to long-winded presentations for fear of getting derailed by others' comments. He set himself a "no PowerPoint" rule to develop a more relaxed, improvisational style. He surprised himself by how much he learned, not only about his own evolving preferences but also about the issues at hand.

Don't stick to "your story"

Most of us have personal narratives about defining moments that taught us important lessons. Consciously or not, we allow our stories, and the images of ourselves that they paint, to guide us in new situations. But the stories can become outdated as we grow, so sometimes it's necessary to alter them dramatically or even to throw them out and start from scratch.

That was true for Maria, a leader who saw herself as a "mother hen with her chicks all around." Her coach, former Ogilvy & Mather CEO Charlotte Beers, explains in *I'd Rather Be in Charge* that this self-image emerged from a time when Maria had to sacrifice her own goals and dreams to take care of her extended family. It eventually began to hold her back in her career: Though it had worked for her as a friendly and loyal team player and a peacekeeper, it wasn't helping her get the big leadership assignment she wanted. Together Maria and her coach looked for another defining moment to use as a touch-stone—one that was more in keeping with Maria's desired future self, not who she had been in the past. They chose the time when Maria, as a young woman, had left her family to travel the world for 18 months. Acting from that bolder sense of self, she asked for—and got—a promotion that had previously been elusive.

Dan McAdams, a Northwestern psychology professor who has spent his career studying life stories, describes identity as "the internalized and evolving story that results from a person's selective appropriation of past, present and future." This isn't just academic jargon. McAdams is saying that you have to believe your story—but also embrace how it changes over time, according to what you need it to do. Try out new stories about yourself, and keep editing them, much as you would your résumé.

Again, revising one's story is both an introspective and a social process. The narratives we choose should not only sum up our experiences and aspirations but also reflect the demands we face and resonate with the audience we're trying to win over.

———————

Countless books and advisers tell you to start your leadership journey with a clear sense of who you are. But that can be a recipe for staying stuck in the past. Your leadership identity can and should change each time you move on to bigger and better things.

The only way we grow as leaders is by stretching the limits of who we are—doing new things that make us uncomfortable but that teach us through direct experience who we want to become. Such growth doesn't require a radical personality makeover. Small changes—in the way we carry ourselves, the way we communicate, the way we interact—often make a world of difference in how effectively we lead.

Originally published in January–February 2015. Reprint R1501C

The Discipline of Business Experimentation

by Stefan Thomke and Jim Manzi

SOON AFTER RON JOHNSON left Apple to become the CEO of J.C. Penney, in 2011, his team implemented a bold plan that eliminated coupons and clearance racks, filled stores with branded boutiques, and used technology to eliminate cashiers, cash registers, and checkout counters. Yet just 17 months after Johnson joined Penney, sales had plunged, losses had soared, and Johnson had lost his job. The retailer then did an about-face.

How could Penney have gone so wrong? Didn't it have tons of transaction data revealing customers' tastes and preferences?

Presumably it did, but the problem is that big data can provide clues only about the past behavior of customers—not about how they will react to bold changes. When it comes to innovation, then, most managers must operate in a world where they lack sufficient data to inform their decisions. Consequently, they often rely on their experience or intuition. But ideas that are truly innovative—that is, those that can reshape industries—typically go against the grain of executive experience and conventional wisdom.

Managers can, however, discover whether a new product or business program will succeed by subjecting it to a rigorous test. Think of it this way: A pharmaceutical company would never introduce a drug without first conducting a round of experiments based on established scientific protocols. (In fact, the U.S. Food and Drug Administration requires extensive clinical trials.) Yet that's essentially what many companies do when they roll out new business models and other novel concepts. Had J.C. Penney done thorough experiments on its CEO's proposed changes, the company might have discovered that customers would probably reject them.

Why don't more companies conduct rigorous tests of their risky overhauls and expensive proposals? Because most organizations are reluctant to fund proper business experiments and have considerable difficulty executing them. Although the process of experimentation seems straightforward, it is surprisingly hard in practice, owing to myriad organizational and technical challenges. That is the overarching conclusion of our 40-plus years of collective experience conducting and studying business experiments at dozens of companies, including Bank of America, BMW, Hilton, Kraft, Petco, Staples, Subway, and Walmart.

Running a standard A/B test over a direct channel such as the internet—comparing, for instance, the response rate to version A of a web page with the response rate to version B—is a relatively uncomplicated exercise using math developed a century ago. But the vast majority (more than 90%) of consumer business is conducted through more-complex distribution systems, such as store networks, sales territories, bank branches, fast-food franchises, and so on. Business experimentation in such environments suffers from a variety of analytical complexities, the most important of which is that sample sizes are typically too small to yield valid results. Whereas a large online retailer can simply select 50,000 consumers in a random fashion and determine their reactions to an experimental offering, even the largest brick-and-mortar retailers can't randomly assign 50,000 stores to test a new promotion. For them, a realistic test group usually numbers in the dozens, not the thousands. Indeed, we have found that most tests of new consumer programs are too informal. They are not based on proven scientific and statistical methods, and so executives end up misinterpreting statistical noise as causation—and making bad decisions.

Idea in Brief

The Problem

In the absence of sufficient data to inform decisions about proposed innovations, managers often rely on their experience, intuition, or conventional wisdom—none of which is necessarily relevant.

The Solution

A rigorous scientific test, in which companies separate an independent variable (the presumed cause) from a dependent variable (the observed effect) while holding all other potential causes constant, and then manipulate the former to study changes in the latter.

The Guidance

To make the most of their experiments, companies must ask: Does the experiment have a clear purpose? Have stakeholders made a commitment to abide by the results? Is the experiment doable? How can we ensure reliable results? Have we gotten the most value out of the experiment?

In an ideal experiment the tester separates an independent variable (the presumed cause) from a dependent variable (the observed effect) while holding all other potential causes constant, and then manipulates the former to study changes in the latter. The manipulation, followed by careful observation and analysis, yields insight into the relationships between cause and effect, which ideally can be applied to and tested in other settings.

To obtain that kind of knowledge—and ensure that business experimentation is worth the expense and effort—companies need to ask themselves several crucial questions: Does the experiment have a clear purpose? Have stakeholders made a commitment to abide by the results? Is the experiment doable? How can we ensure reliable results? Have we gotten the most value out of the experiment? (See the sidebar "Checklist for Running a Business Experiment.") Although those questions seem obvious, many companies begin conducting tests without fully addressing them.

Does the Experiment Have a Clear Purpose?

Companies should conduct experiments if they are the only practical way to answer specific questions about proposed management actions.

Checklist for Running a Business Experiment

Purpose

- Does the experiment focus on a specific management action under consideration?
- What do people hope to learn from the experiment?

Buy-In

- What specific changes would be made on the basis of the results?
- How will the organization ensure that the results aren't ignored?
- How does the experiment fit into the organization's overall learning agenda and strategic priorities?

Feasibility

- Does the experiment have a testable prediction?
- What is the required sample size? Note: The sample size will depend on the expected effect (for example, a 5% increase in sales).
- Can the organization feasibly conduct the experiment at the test locations for the required duration?

Consider Kohl's, the large retailer, which in 2013 was looking for ways to decrease its operating costs. One suggestion was to open stores an hour later on Monday through Saturday. Company executives were split on the matter. Some argued that reducing the stores' hours would result in a significant drop in sales; others claimed that the impact on sales would be minimal. The only way to settle the debate with any certainty was to conduct a rigorous experiment. A test involving 100 of the company's stores showed that the delayed opening would not result in any meaningful sales decline.

In determining whether an experiment is needed, managers must first figure out exactly what they want to learn. Only then can they decide if testing is the best approach and, if it is, the scope of the experiment. In the case of Kohl's, the hypothesis to be tested was

Reliability

- What measures will be used to account for systemic bias, whether it's conscious or unconscious?
- Do the characteristics of the control group match those of the test group?
- Can the experiment be conducted in either "blind" or "double-blind" fashion?
- Have any remaining biases been eliminated through statistical analyses or other techniques?
- Would others conducting the same test obtain similar results?

Value

- Has the organization considered a targeted rollout—that is, one that takes into account a proposed initiative's effect on different customers, markets, and segments—to concentrate investments in areas where the potential payback is highest?
- Has the organization implemented only the components of an initiative with the highest return on investment?
- Does the organization have a better understanding of what variables are causing what effects?

straightforward: Opening stores an hour later to reduce operating costs will not lead to a significant drop in sales. All too often, though, companies lack the discipline to hone their hypotheses, leading to tests that are inefficient, unnecessarily costly, or, worse, ineffective in answering the question at hand. A weak hypothesis (such as "We can extend our brand upmarket") doesn't present a specific independent variable to test on a specific dependent variable, so it is difficult either to support or to reject. A good hypothesis helps delineate those variables.

In many situations executives need to go beyond the direct effects of an initiative and investigate its ancillary effects. For example, when Family Dollar wanted to determine whether to invest in refrigeration units so that it could sell eggs, milk, and other perishables, it discovered that a side effect—the increase in the sales of traditional dry goods to the additional customers drawn to the stores by the refrigerated items—would actually have a bigger impact on profits. Ancillary effects can also be negative. A few years ago, Wawa, the convenience store chain in the mid-Atlantic United States, wanted to introduce a flatbread breakfast item that had done well in spot tests. But the initiative was killed before the launch, when a rigorous experiment—complete with test and control groups followed by regression analyses—showed that the new product would likely cannibalize other more profitable items.

Have Stakeholders Made a Commitment to Abide by the Results?

Before conducting any test, stakeholders must agree how they'll proceed once the results are in. They should promise to weigh all the findings instead of cherry-picking data that supports a particular point of view. Perhaps most important, they must be willing to walk away from a project if it's not supported by the data.

When Kohl's was considering adding a new product category, furniture, many executives were tremendously enthusiastic, anticipating significant additional revenue. A test at 70 stores over six months, however, showed a net *decrease* in revenue. Products that now had less floor space (to make room for the furniture) experienced a drop in sales, and Kohl's was actually losing customers overall. Those negative results were a huge disappointment for those who had advocated for the initiative, but the program was nevertheless scrapped. The Kohl's example highlights the fact that experiments are often needed to perform objective assessments of initiatives backed by people with organizational clout.

Of course, there might be good reasons for rolling out an initiative even when the anticipated benefits are not supported by the data—for example, a program that experiments have shown will not substantially boost sales might still be necessary to build customer loyalty. But if the proposed initiative is a done deal, why go through the time and expense of conducting a test?

A process should be instituted to ensure that test results aren't ignored, even when they contradict the assumptions or intuition of top executives. At Publix Super Markets, a chain in the southeastern United States, virtually all large retail projects, especially those requiring considerable capital expenditures, must undergo formal experiments to receive a green light. Proposals go through a filtering process in which the first step is for finance to perform an analysis to determine if an experiment is worth conducting.

For projects that make the cut, analytics professionals develop test designs and submit them to a committee that includes the vice president of finance. The experiments approved by the committee are then conducted and overseen by an internal test group. Finance will approve significant expenditures only for proposed initiatives that have adhered to this process and whose experiment results are positive. "Projects get reviewed and approved much more quickly—and with less scrutiny—when they have our test results to back them," says Frank Maggio, the senior manager of business analysis at Publix.

When constructing and implementing such a filtering process, it is important to remember that experiments should be part of a learning agenda that supports a firm's organizational priorities. At Petco each test request must address how that particular experiment would contribute to the company's overall strategy to become more innovative. In the past the company performed about 100 tests a year, but that number has been trimmed to 75. Many test requests are denied because the company has done a similar test in the past; others are rejected because the changes under consideration are not radical enough to justify the expense of testing (for example, a price increase of a single item from $2.79 to $2.89). "We want to test things that will grow the business," says John Rhoades, the company's former director of retail analytics. "We want to try new concepts or new ideas."

Is the Experiment Doable?

Experiments must have testable predictions. But the "causal density" of the business environment—that is, the complexity of the variables and their interactions—can make it extremely difficult to determine cause-and-effect relationships. Learning from a business experiment is not necessarily as easy as isolating an independent variable, manipulating it, and observing changes in the dependent variable. Environments are constantly changing, the potential causes of business outcomes are often uncertain or unknown, and so linkages between them are frequently complex and poorly understood.

Consider a hypothetical retail chain that has 10,000 convenience stores, 8,000 of which are named QwikMart and 2,000 FastMart. The QwikMart stores have been averaging $1 million in annual sales and the FastMart stores $1.1 million. A senior executive asks a seemingly simple question: Would changing the name of the QwikMart stores to FastMart lead to an increase in revenue of $800 million? Obviously, numerous factors affect store sales, including the physical size of the store, the number of people who live within a certain radius and their average incomes, the number of hours the store is open per week, the experience of the store manager, the number of nearby competitors, and so on. But the executive is interested in just one variable: the stores' name (QwikMart versus FastMart).

The obvious solution is to conduct an experiment by changing the name of a handful of QwikMart stores (say, 10) to see what happens. But even determining the effect of the name change on those stores turns out to be tricky, because many other variables may have changed at the same time. For example, the weather was very bad at four of the locations, a manager was replaced in one, a large residential building opened near another, and a competitor started an aggressive advertising promotion near yet another. Unless the company can isolate the effect of the name change from those and other variables, the executive won't know for sure whether the name change has helped (or hurt) business.

To deal with environments of high causal density, companies need to consider whether it's feasible to use a sample large enough to average out the effects of all variables except those being studied. Unfortunately, that type of experiment is not always doable. The cost of a test involving an adequate sample size might be prohibitive, or the change in operations could be too disruptive. In such instances, as we discuss later, executives can sometimes employ sophisticated analytical techniques, some involving big data, to increase the statistical validity of their results.

That said, it should be noted that managers often mistakenly assume that a larger sample will automatically lead to better data. Indeed, an experiment can involve a lot of observations, but if they are highly clustered, or correlated to one another, then the true sample size might actually be quite small. When a company uses a distributor instead of selling directly to customers, for example, that distribution point could easily lead to correlations among customer data.

The required sample size depends in large part on the magnitude of the expected effect. If a company expects the cause (for example, a change in store name) to have a large effect (a substantial increase in sales), the sample can be smaller. If the expected effect is small, the sample must be larger. This might seem counterintuitive, but think of it this way: The smaller the expected effect, the greater the number of observations that are required to detect it from the surrounding noise with the desired statistical confidence.

Selecting the right sample size does more than ensure that the results will be statistically valid; it can also enable a company to decrease testing costs and increase innovation. Readily available software programs can help companies choose the optimal sample size. (Full disclosure: Jim Manzi's firm, Applied Predictive Technologies, sells one, Test & Learn.)

How Can We Ensure Reliable Results?

In the previous section we described the basics for conducting an experiment. However, the truth is that companies typically have to make trade-offs between reliability, cost, time, and other practical considerations. Three methods can help reduce the trade-offs, thus increasing the reliability of the results.

Randomized field trials
The concept of randomization in medical research is simple: Take a large group of individuals with the same characteristics and affliction, and randomly divide them into two subgroups. Administer

the treatment to just one subgroup and closely monitor everyone's health. If the treated (or test) group does statistically better than the untreated (or control) group, then the therapy is deemed to be effective. Similarly, randomized field trials can help companies determine whether specific changes will lead to improved performance.

The financial services company Capital One has long used rigorous experiments to test even the most seemingly trivial changes. Through randomized field trials, for instance, the company might test the color of the envelopes used for product offers by sending out two batches (one in the test color and the other in white) to determine any differences in response.

Randomization plays an important role: It helps prevent systemic bias, introduced consciously or unconsciously, from affecting an experiment, and it evenly spreads any remaining (and possibly unknown) potential causes of the outcome between the test and control groups. But randomized field tests are not without challenges. For the results to be valid, the field trials must be conducted in a statistically rigorous fashion.

Instead of identifying a population of test subjects with the same characteristics and then randomly dividing it into two groups, managers sometimes make the mistake of selecting a test group (say, a group of stores in a chain) and then assuming that everything else (the remainder of the stores) should be the control group. Or they select the test and control groups in ways that inadvertently introduce biases into the experiment. Petco used to select its 30 best stores to try out a new initiative (as a test group) and compare them with its 30 worst stores (as the control group). Initiatives tested in this way would often look very promising but fail when they were rolled out.

Now Petco considers a wide range of parameters—store size, customer demographics, the presence of nearby competitors, and so on—to match the characteristics of the control and test groups. (Publix does the same.) The results from those experiments have been much more reliable.

Blind tests

To minimize biases and increase reliability further, Petco and Publix have conducted "blind" tests, which help prevent the Hawthorne effect: the tendency of study participants to modify their behavior, consciously or subconsciously, when they are aware that they are part of an experiment. At Petco none of the test stores' staffers know when experiments are under way, and Publix conducts blind tests whenever it can. For simple tests involving price changes, Publix can use blind procedures because stores are continually rolling out new prices, so the tests are indistinguishable from normal operating practices.

But blind procedures are not always practical. For tests of new equipment or work practices, Publix typically informs the stores that have been selected for the test group. (Note: A higher experimental standard is the use of "double-blind" tests, in which neither the experimenters nor the test subjects are aware of which participants are in the test group and which are in the control. Double-blind tests are widely used in medical research but are not commonplace in business experimentation.)

Big data

In online and other direct-channel environments, the math required to conduct a rigorous randomized experiment is well known. But as we discussed earlier, the vast majority of consumer transactions occur in other channels, such as retail stores. In tests in such environments, sample sizes are often smaller than 100, violating typical assumptions of many standard statistical methods. To minimize the effects of this limitation, companies can utilize specialized algorithms in combination with multiple sets of big data (see the sidebar "How Big Data Can Help").

Consider a large retailer contemplating a store redesign that was going to cost a half-billion dollars to roll out to 1,300 locations. To test the idea, the retailer redesigned 20 stores and tracked the results. The finance team analyzed the data and concluded that the upgrade would increase sales by a meager 0.5%, resulting in a negative return

How Big Data Can Help

TO FILTER OUT statistical noise and identify cause-and-effect relationships, business experiments should ideally employ samples numbering in the thousands. But this can be prohibitively expensive or impossible. A new approach to merchandise assortment may have to be tested in just 25 stores, a sales-training program with 32 salespeople, and a proposed remodeling in 10 hotel properties. In such situations, big data and other sophisticated computing techniques, such as "machine learning," can help. Here's how:

Getting Started

If a retailer wants to test a new store layout, it should collect detailed data (such as competitors' proximity, employees' tenures, and customer demography) about each unit of analysis (each store and its trade area, each salesperson and her accounts, and so on). This will become part of a big data set. Determining how many and which stores, customers, or employees should be part of the test and how long the test should run depends on the volatility in the data and the precision required for impact estimates.

Building a Control Group

In experiments involving small samples, correctly matching test subjects (such as individual stores or customers) to control subjects is essential and depends on the experimenter's ability to fully identify dozens or even hundreds of variables that characterize the test subjects. Big data feeds (complete transaction logs by customer, detailed weather data, social media streams, and so on) can

---

on investment. The marketing team conducted a separate analysis and forecast that the redesign would lead to a healthy 5% sales increase.

As it turned out, the finance team had compared the test sites with other stores in the chain that were of similar size, demographic income, and other variables but were not necessarily in the same geographic market. It had also used data six months before and after the redesign. In contrast, the marketing team had compared stores within the same geographic region and had considered data 12 months before and after the redesign. To determine which results to trust, the company employed big data, including transaction-level data (store items, the times of day when the sale occurred, prices), store attributes, and data on the environments around the stores assist in this. Once the characteristics are determined, a control group can be built that contains all elements of the test group except for what is being tested. This allows the retailer to determine whether the test results were influenced only by that one element—the new layout—or by other factors (demographic variances, better economic conditions, warmer weather).

Targeting the Best Opportunities

The same data feeds can be used to identify situations in which the tested program is effective. For example, the new store layout may work better in highly competitive urban areas but may be only moderately successful in other markets. By pinpointing these patterns, the experimenter can implement the program in situations where it works and avoid investments where the program may not generate the best ROI.

Tailoring the Program

Additional large data feeds can be used to characterize program components that are more or less effective. For example, a retailer testing the effects of a new store layout can use data captured from in-store video streams to determine whether the new layout is encouraging customers to move through more of the store or is generating more traffic near high-margin products. Or the experimenter may find that moving items to the front of the store and putting in new shelves have a positive impact, but moving the sales registers disrupts checkouts and hurts profits.

(competition, demographics, weather). In this way, the company selected stores for the control group that were a closer match with those in which the redesign was tested, which made the small sample size statistically valid. It then used objective, statistical methods to review both analyses. The results: The marketing team's findings were the more accurate of the two.

Even when a company can't follow a rigorous testing protocol, analysts can help identify and correct for certain biases, randomization failures, and other experimental imperfections. A common situation is when an organization's testing function is presented with nonrandomized natural experiments—the vice president of operations, for example, might want to know if the company's new employee training program, which was introduced in about 10% of the company's markets, is more effective than the old one. As it turns out, in such situations the same algorithms and big data sets that can be used to address the problem of small or correlated samples can also be deployed to tease out valuable insights and minimize uncertainty in the results. The analysis can then help experimenters design a true randomized field trial to confirm and refine the results, especially when they are somewhat counterintuitive or are needed to inform a decision with large economic stakes.

For any experiment, the gold standard is repeatability; that is, others conducting the same test should obtain similar results. Repeating an expensive test is usually impractical, but companies can verify results in other ways. Petco sometimes deploys a staged rollout for large initiatives to confirm the results before proceeding with a companywide implementation. And Publix has a process for tracking the results of a rollout and comparing them with the predicted benefit.

Have We Gotten the Most Value out of the Experiment?

Many companies go through the expense of conducting experiments but then fail to make the most of them. To avoid that mistake, executives should take into account a proposed initiative's effect on various customers, markets, and segments and concentrate investments in areas where the potential paybacks are highest. The correct question is usually not, What works? but, What works where?

Petco frequently rolls out a program only in stores that are most similar to the test stores that had the best results. By doing so, Petco not only saves on implementation costs but also avoids involving stores where the new program might not deliver benefits or might even have negative consequences. Thanks to such targeted rollouts, Petco has consistently been able to double the predicted benefits of new initiatives.

Another useful tactic is "value engineering." Most programs have some components that create benefits in excess of costs and others that do not. The trick, then, is to implement just the components with an attractive return on investment (ROI). As a simple example, let's say that a retailer's tests of a 20%-off promotion show a 5% lift in sales. What portion of that increase was due to the offer itself and what resulted from the accompanying advertising and training of store staff, both of which directed customers to those particular sales products? In such cases, companies can conduct experiments to investigate various combinations of components (for instance, the promotional offer with advertising but without additional staff training). An analysis of the results can disentangle the effects, allowing executives to drop the components (say, the additional staff training) that have a low or negative ROI.

Moreover, a careful analysis of data generated by experiments can enable companies to better understand their operations and test their assumptions of which variables cause which effects. With big data, the emphasis is on correlation—discovering, for instance, that sales of certain products tend to coincide with sales of others. But business experimentation can allow companies to look beyond correlation and investigate causality—uncovering, for instance, the factors causing the increase (or decrease) of purchases. Such fundamental knowledge of causality can be crucial. Without it, executives have only a fragmentary understanding of their businesses, and the decisions they make can easily backfire.

When Cracker Barrel Old Country Store, the Southern-themed restaurant chain, conducted an experiment to determine whether it should switch from incandescent to LED lights at its restaurants, executives were astonished to learn that customer traffic actually *decreased* in the locations that installed LED lights. The lighting initiative could have stopped there, but the company dug deeper to understand the underlying causes. As it turned out, the new lighting made the front porches of the restaurants look dimmer, and many customers mistakenly thought that the restaurants were closed. This was puzzling—the LEDs should have made the porches brighter. Upon further investigation, executives learned that the store managers hadn't previously been following the company's lighting standards; they had been making their own adjustments, often adding extra lighting on the front porches. And so the luminosity dropped when the stores adhered to the new LED policy. The point here is that correlation alone would have left the company with the wrong impression—that LEDs are bad for business. It took experimentation to uncover the actual causal relationship.

Indeed, without fully understanding causality, companies leave themselves open to making big mistakes. Remember the experiment Kohl's did to investigate the effects of delaying the opening of its stores? During that testing, the company suffered an initial drop in sales. At that point, executives could have pulled the plug on the initiative. But an analysis showed that the number of customer transactions had remained the same; the issue was a drop in units per transaction. Eventually, the units per transaction recovered and total sales returned to previous levels. Kohl's couldn't fully explain the initial decrease, but executives resisted the temptation to blame the reduced operating hours. They didn't rush to equate correlation with causation.

What's important here is that many companies are discovering that conducting an experiment is just the beginning. Value comes from analyzing and then exploiting the data. In the past, Publix spent 80% of its testing time gathering data and 20% analyzing it. The company's current goal is to reverse that ratio.

Challenging Conventional Wisdom

By paying attention to sample sizes, control groups, randomization, and other factors, companies can ensure the validity of their test results. The more valid and repeatable the results, the better they will hold up in the face of internal resistance, which can be especially strong when the results challenge long-standing industry practices and conventional wisdom.

When Petco executives investigated new pricing for a product sold by weight, the results were unequivocal. By far, the best price was for a quarter pound of the product, and that price was for an amount that ended in $.25. That result went sharply against the grain of conventional wisdom, which typically calls for prices ending in 9, such as $4.99 or $2.49. "This broke a rule in retailing that you can't have an 'ugly' price," notes Rhoades. At first, executives at

Petco were skeptical of the results, but because the experiment had been conducted so rigorously, they eventually were willing to give the new pricing a try. A targeted rollout confirmed the results, leading to a sales jump of more than 24% after six months.

The lesson is not merely that business experimentation can lead to better ways of doing things. It can also give companies the confidence to overturn wrongheaded conventional wisdom and the faulty business intuition that even seasoned executives can display. And smarter decision making ultimately leads to improved performance.

Could J.C. Penney have averted disaster by rigorously testing the components of its overhaul? At this point, it's impossible to know. But one thing's for certain: Before attempting to implement such a bold program, the company needed to make sure that knowledge—not just intuition—was guiding the decision.

Originally published in December 2014. Reprint R1412D

When Senior Managers Won't Collaborate

by Heidi K. Gardner

TODAY'S PROFESSIONAL SERVICES FIRMS face a conundrum. As clients have globalized and confronted more-sophisticated technological, regulatory, economic, and environmental demands, they've sought help on increasingly complex problems. To keep up, most top-tier firms have created or acquired narrowly defined practice areas and encouraged partners to specialize. As a result, their collective expertise has been distributed across more and more people, places, and practice groups. The only way to address clients' most complex issues, then, is for specialists to work together across the boundaries of their expertise.

When they do, my research shows, their firms earn higher margins, inspire greater client loyalty, and gain a competitive edge. But for the professionals involved, the financial benefits of collaboration accrue slowly, and other advantages are hard to quantify. That makes it difficult to decide whether the investment in learning to collaborate will pay off. Even if they value the camaraderie of collaborative work, many partners are hard-pressed to spend time and energy on cross-specialty ventures when they could be building their own practices instead.

And no wonder. This kind of collaboration is difficult. It's different from mere assembly (in which experts make individual contributions and someone pulls them all together) and from sequential, interdependent projects (in which a professional adds to a piece of work and then hands it over to the next person to work on). It's much harder than simply delegating to junior staffers. It's also not the same as cross-selling, when partner A introduces partner B to her own client so that B can provide additional services. True multidisciplinary collaboration requires people to combine their perspectives and expertise and tailor them to the client's needs so that the outcome is more than the sum of the participating individuals' knowledge.

If professionals better understood the trade-offs, and if firms lowered the organizational barriers to collaboration, then not only clients but also the professionals themselves and their firms would benefit handsomely. My research examines these trade-offs through quantitative analyses of a decade's worth of detailed financial and time-sheet records at three global law firms and one accounting firm, case studies of professional services incumbents and new entrants, and surveys and interviews with hundreds of professionals in a range of sectors, including consulting, law, accounting, engineering, real estate brokerage, architecture, and executive search. (For more details, see the sidebar "About the Research.") My findings show how the benefits of collaboration play out. They paint a realistic picture of the barriers that often prevent professionals from working together. And they suggest changes that both individuals and firms can make to reap more of the advantages and avoid more of the drawbacks.

The Benefits to the Firm

For a firm, the financial benefits of multidisciplinary collaboration are unambiguous. Simply put, the more disciplines that are involved in a client engagement, the greater the annual average revenue the client generates, my research shows. That's in part because cross-specialty work is likely to be less subject to price-based competition. Whereas clients view an engagement involving single-specialty

Idea in Brief

The Problem

Professional services firms can gain a powerful competitive edge if they do complex work for clients that involves partners from multiple specialties. But collaboration's downsides are immediate, while the benefits accrue slowly, making individuals reluctant to engage in it.

The Research

Research shows that as more practice groups work together on a client engagement, the average annual revenue from the client increases. And as professionals engage in more cross-specialty projects, the more work they will subsequently get and the more they'll be able to charge for it.

The Implications

Both individuals and leaders can lower the barriers to collaboration—and land high-value work—by de-emphasizing inputs like billable hours and focusing more on outcomes such as greater revenue per client.

---

expertise (about a basic tax issue, for instance) as a commodity that can be awarded to the lowest bidder, they know that cross-specialty work is complex and harder. As additional practice groups serve a client, the firm can bill a higher amount, and each group earns more, on average. This suggests that the practice groups are collaborating to create additional value, not merely cross-selling discrete services. My research at one global law firm showed rising revenue per client even as five, six, and seven disciplines became involved. (See the exhibit "More collaborators, more revenue.")

I also found that client projects involving offices in several countries are significantly more lucrative than single-office engagements. (See the exhibit "More countries, more revenue.") That's because cross-border work is often especially complex and demanding—think, for example, of issues that arise when multinational companies merge or of the multiple jurisdictions that can be involved in litigation resulting from an oil spill. Delivering seamless service across national boundaries can be an important differentiator for firms.

Moreover, moving beyond siloed services to complex, interdependent engagements allows a professional services firm to work for more-senior executives in a client's organization, who have a greater

About the Research

TO UNDERSTAND WHAT HAPPENS when partners from different special-ties collaborate, I conducted a long-term study in six global professional ser-vices firms in the fields of law, consulting, and accounting. I analyzed more than a decade's worth of time-sheet records in four of the firms to measure the extent and nature of partners' collaboration patterns. In addition, I stud-ied another consulting firm for more than two years as the leaders initiated a strategic change aimed at moving from highly individualistic to more-col-laborative work. Several rounds of surveys tracked hundreds of partners' re-actions to the change over time, and interviews with executives, partners, board members, and clients helped me develop insights into the leadership challenges associated with such initiatives. Further, over the past two years I have conducted more than 150 in-depth interviews with professionals in more than 40 firms to examine the causes and effects of collaboration.

To uncover ways to surmount the barriers to collaboration, I have spoken to more than 2,000 partner-level professionals in the past year, including participants of the Leading Professional Service Firms and Leading Law Firms executive educa-tion courses at Harvard Business School and Harvard Law School; partners in firms that have invited me to conduct collaboration workshops; and firm leaders in small colloquia that I organize specifically to discuss my findings.

span of responsibility and greater authority and budget to hire exter-nal advisers. In the long term, engaging these executives through multidisciplinary projects builds loyalty by creating switching bar-riers. As the general counsel of a *Fortune* 100 company explained, "I could find a decent tax lawyer in most firms. But when a tax law-yer successfully teamed up with an intellectual property lawyer, a regulatory lawyer, and ultimately a litigator to handle my thorni-est patent issues, I knew I could never replace that whole team in another firm."

From an organizational perspective, the more partners who serve a given client, the more likely that client is to become "institutional-ized"—owned, as it were, by the firm rather than controlled by one partner—reducing the risk that a departing professional will take that client with her. What's more, partners' ability to see their col-leagues' work lowers the risk of illicit rogue behavior (something that is admittedly rare but can be fatal).

More collaborators, more revenue

As more practice groups collaborate to serve a client, the average annual revenue from the client increases, over and above what each practice would have earned from selling discrete services.

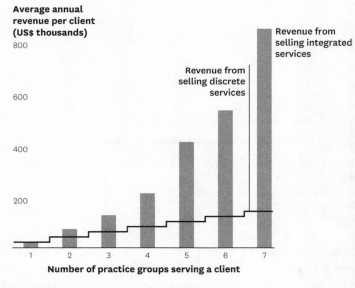

Average annual revenue per client (US$ thousands)

Revenue from selling integrated services

Revenue from selling discrete services

Number of practice groups serving a client

Source: Heidi K. Gardner, data from a global law firm

How Individuals Benefit

The benefits of collaboration to individuals are equally quantifiable, if less intuitive. My research clearly shows that professionals who contribute to colleagues' client work sell more services to their own clients. Why? When you team up with colleagues, they better understand what you have to offer, and that knowledge makes them more likely to refer work to you down the road. Because referrals are a more-efficient way to generate work than prospecting on your own, they make it easier to reach revenue targets. In one law firm I studied, a single work referral typically generated about $50,000 of extra revenue for the partner who received it.

More countries, more revenue

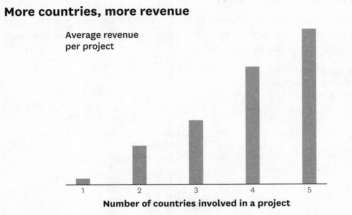

Average revenue per project

Number of countries involved in a project

As the number of countries involved in a client project increases, so does revenue.

Source: Heidi K. Gardner, data from a global law firm

Of course, not all colleagues who come to appreciate your capabilities will send you work immediately; they must wait until their clients require your expertise. On average, partners in my study got a new client referral within a year from one in every six colleagues they teamed up with.

But even when teammates don't send work themselves, they are likely to spread word of your expertise to colleagues who need it. At the law firm, it took working with just two extra teammates to generate a referral from someone who had never sent work to that individual before. That might not seem like much, but the compounded effect of word of mouth is powerful: As colleagues recommend your work to others in the firm, your reputation is likely to grow significantly over time.

Collaboration raises a partner's profile not only with colleagues but also in the wider market. Professional services are notoriously opaque: It's hard for clients to judge their value, even after the fact. At least in the near term, it's nearly impossible to answer with any certainty questions like "Did the consultant's recommendation lead to our bankruptcy?" "Did the executive search firm place the absolute best candidate in the role?" or "What risks would we have faced without the vast legal expenditure?" That uncertainty means that clients rely heavily on a professional's reputation, gleaned from word-of-mouth recommendations, when making hiring decisions. Those recommendations carry a lot of weight; they lead not only to more work but also to more-sophisticated and more-lucrative work. At the law firm, the more cross–discipline projects partners worked on, and the more complex each one was, the more partners could charge for their work in subsequent years.

Working on multidisciplinary projects also helps professionals learn how to sell more-sophisticated work to their own clients. Take Laurie, a consultant specializing in operations efficiency for automotive clients. Two years ago she was drawn onto a postmerger integration project for a pharmaceutical company because many of her colleagues in the operations practice had conflicts of interest. Laurie was introduced to the frameworks and approaches used by her colleagues in finance, regulation, and branding, and she began to understand how those disciplines informed one another. With these new lenses, she could spot a broader array of issues for her own clients. Laurie stayed in touch with several of the experts from other specialty areas, and their informal talks bolstered her ability to strike up conversations with her clients about issues beyond operations. Some 18 months later one of her automotive clients engaged Laurie's firm for a wholesale restructuring of a division, and Laurie is now leading the cross-practice team.

Complex projects give individuals access to those high-level executives in the client organization who have more responsibility and larger budgets. One chief executive I spoke with recalled a consultant he had worked with earlier in his career. This consultant, a marketing specialist, tended to focus exclusively on brand-related issues in her clients' product portfolios, and so her influence never extended beyond the marketing department. The CEO contrasted her with one of his current consultants, who drew on cross-specialty experience to recognize that the company's product portfolio affected its offshoring operations and in turn its tax regime. This savvy consultant identified a complex project involving not only marketing but also operations, strategy, and finance experts. The project commanded higher fees, and the consultant established a reputation as a go-to person for sophisticated issues.

Cross-disciplinary collaboration also helps insulate professionals from economic downturns. I found that professionals who were even moderately connected to others in their firm—that is, they had worked each year with just 10 other partners in the three years prior to the 2008 recession—preserved their revenue during the downturn, whereas the revenue of those who were more isolated dropped significantly. And collaborating partners' revenue climbed much more quickly when the economy recovered. Some of this benefit derives from the social cohesion that stems from collaboration: Those who had teamed up before the downturn were more likely to continue spreading their client work even when the total amount dwindled. In addition, by working on multipractice projects in flush times, professionals learned to handle a broader set of topics, diluting the risk that their own specialty would get hammered during hard times.

What Gets in the Way

As compelling as this evidence is, it's no secret that the organizational structure, compensation systems, and cultures in many, if not most, professional services firms favor individual contributors rather than team players. Up-or-out promotion systems encourage rivalry among junior associates, and the competitive values become so ingrained that the winners find it counterintuitive to collaborate when they become partners.

Moreover, as one partner quipped, many firms value "rock stars, not the whole band." The rainmakers are often the most celebrated people in a firm. They're frequently rewarded with something akin to a commission—a percentage of their gross sales. In some firms the higher your revenue, the higher the percentage. The simplicity of these compensation models can be an advantage—people know exactly what they need to do and how much they'll make in return. But they discourage collaboration, because professionals who bring in a colleague to close a deal will need to split the commission.

The effects of the compensation system bleed into the culture, which disparages "service partners," who contribute primarily by delivering work on others' projects. As one COO explained, partners often believe that "some people are rainmakers, but others just get wet." In this environment, partners who try their hand at collaborating can be hit hard. Consider a firm that celebrates individual sales performance by inducting qualifiers into the "Million Dollar Club" at its annual banquet. A partner described applauding his colleagues through gritted teeth one year when he had missed the million-dollar target because he'd shared most of his client origination credits with junior colleagues who were struggling to build their own client rosters. "I thought I'd done exactly what the CEO wanted by mentoring those rookies and splitting the credit with them," he said. "But it was the only year I wasn't called up on stage at our annual meeting, and I'll never do it again."

And to be honest, some of the advantages firms gain from collaboration may come at the expense of individuals. The increased transparency, for instance, can feel from the professionals' point of view like heightened scrutiny over their client dealings and an infringement on their autonomy. What's more, many professional services firms ask applicants to assess the number of and associated fees from clients they anticipate would follow them. Once a professional can no longer claim that clients would necessarily come along if he left for a competitor, he loses his bargaining power not only in the firm but also in the marketplace.

External reward systems also play a role in encouraging professionals to develop a reputation for specialized expertise. For example, in public "star ranking" systems *Chambers USA* designates the nation's premier lawyers, and *Institutional Investor* recognizes the best equity analysts. These ratings influence a professional's income, attractiveness in the labor market, and career advancement, and some professionals worry that working on cross-discipline projects will cut their chances of gaining recognition.

As if these financial concerns weren't enough, learning to collaborate effectively is difficult. Few professionals truly work alone, but coordinating with peers across departments is significantly harder than delegating to junior staffers in your own department whose skills are similar (but inferior) to your own, and whose advancement depends on pleasing you. To acquire more-sophisticated work, professionals must learn how to determine what a client needs beyond what they can offer; find people who can serve those needs; learn to work with high-powered peers over whom they have no authority; and trust them to be competent at something they're not in a position to judge and not to steal the client away. Work that spans multiple countries raises cross-cultural issues, which pose further challenges.

Getting to the Benefits Sooner

Even in organizations in which these factors are at play, some people are working effectively across disciplines. What these people have figured out is that perseverance pays off. Once they gain some experience with collaboration and develop a cadre of experts whose competence and character they can rely on, the risks decrease, as do the coordination costs. As they learn the jargon, technical approaches, and assumptions of other disciplines and figure out how to share revenue and less tangible rewards (like credit for the outcome or airtime for a subsequent client pitch), they build trust and can work with peers more quickly and with less tension.

Certain strategies can help professionals reap the benefits of collaboration sooner. First, it matters whom you collaborate with. In my research I found that establishing your credentials with a rainmaker or other well-connected colleague who has influence in the firm is simply the most powerful way to enhance your own reputation. And the financial benefits from such a relationship, which come from referrals, build up significantly over the years.

But how can you get yourself onto a project with high-status colleagues? Chris, a partner in the New York office of a global law firm, uses the following tactic: From discussions with colleagues or articles in the legal press, she gleans ideas for how her expertise in data privacy might be useful to various kinds of corporate clients. She then researches companies that her firm already serves and writes a one-page memo to a client relationship partner outlining how her expertise could help that particular client solve a particular problem. Chris admits that the effort takes a lot of time, and not all her colleagues are receptive to what they see as self-promotion. But enough of them have welcomed the offer that she has participated in multiple joint pitches for new work and has established a couple of ongoing relationships with other partners.

Another way to work with influential colleagues is to invite them onto your own client projects. Matthias, a veteran consulting partner, transferred from a boutique telecommunications firm to a generalist firm so he could apply his operations expertise to a wider array of clients. Soon after joining the new firm, he identified three partners who were seen as prime players in other practice groups and invited each to lunch. He then spent hours conducting due diligence—reading their public white papers and the documents they had contributed to the firm's knowledge management system, reading up on their clients, and talking to partners in his own practice who'd worked with them. Within his first year, Matthias found openings to hold joint meetings at his client with each of those partners; one meeting led to a small but promising stream of work. The three partners grew to appreciate Matthias's deep expertise, his client-handling skills, and his intention to stay at the firm and build a thriving business there. Over time, those partners began telling others of their impressions of him, creating opportunities for him on client work across a range of industries. The initial trick, Matthias explained, was to learn enough of the domain expertise of other partners to be able to identify opportunities for them with his own clients and then to start discussions about those opportunities.

You might get high-status partners to work with you on the basis of your knowledge and expertise, but getting them to keep working with you hinges on their experience of you as a team player. None of this is rocket science, but about half the complaints I heard in my interviews would have been eliminated if professionals had followed these rules.

Don't squeeze your team members

If your firm is one in which partners negotiate fees or rates, bend over backwards to be fair to the partners you invite onto your team. Even if your client is more important to the firm than theirs, don't expect them to drop everything to handle your engagement or to throw in their work uncompensated. Credit is another important type of currency, and people are keenly aware of how fairly (or not) it gets divided in teams. Some of the strongest complaints arise about partners who entice others onto a project but then fail to give them any face time with clients, pigeonhole them into areas where they won't shine, fail to acknowledge their contribution—or, worse, take credit for it themselves. Don't waste your colleagues' time by repeatedly changing deadlines. Don't create fire drills by getting people to work all night and then ignoring their input for days. Most partners know better than to treat their peers like this, but they fail to recognize that a reputation for abusing associates' time is also a turnoff for partners who hear about it.

Deliver what you committed to on time, without reminders

Communicate immediately if a real emergency delays you, but don't make excuses, and definitely don't blame underlings. Clarify expectations and your circumstances up front, such as travel plans that will make it hard for teammates to contact you.

Communicate openly

Ask questions. Seek advice freely and offer it tactfully when you see a need. Most people don't like to give negative feedback to their peers. But partners who join you on client work shouldn't have to guess whether their contributions are up to par. If you give people constructive, honest, and timely comments, you'll maximize their ability to learn from your project, which is one of the key benefits individuals gain from collaboration. You'll also build a team of capable, loyal people who can handle complicated projects, which will give you the confidence to pitch such work to clients.

How Rainmakers Profit from Collaboration

TO ILLUSTRATE HOW collaboration enhances a professional's ability to generate business, let's compare two nearly identical lawyers. Both graduated from law school the same year and are in the same practice area at the same firm. They billed nearly the same number of hours in a given year, but it's clear from the diagram that they spent those hours in very different ways. Lawyer 1 brought six other partners into his own client work, half of whom were not from his own practice area (as shown by the gray dots). Lawyer 2 involved more than 30 other partners in work that he generated, two-thirds of them from outside his practice. Lawyer 2's multidisciplinary approach paid off: Total revenue that year from his clients was more than four times higher than revenue from Lawyer 1's.

This simple example can't tell us whether collaboration led to the increased revenue or was a result of it. But my research examining outcomes over a decade shows a clear causal pattern: The more a partner shares work she's originated, the more work she is likely to generate in subsequent years, even controlling for other factors that are likely to affect individual billings, such as one's office, practice group, organizational tenure, and previous year's billings. Subsequent-year revenue from a rainmaker's *existing* clients increases the more she involves partners from both her own and other practices. For *new* clients, cross-practice collaboration is an even stronger predictor of long-term revenue growth.

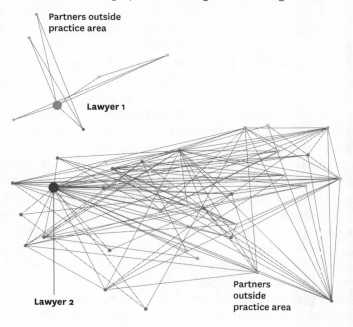

Organizing for Higher-Value Work

Some firms foster high levels of collaboration among even their most powerful, successful professionals. To outsiders it can seem like magic, but leaders in these organizations take two broad approaches that help professionals get over the initial hurdles to effective collaboration: They act as coaches in order to lower cultural barriers, and they act as architects in order to lower structural barriers.

The leader as coach

Leaders who want to build a culture of collaboration should begin with themselves, modeling the right behavior by contributing to others' client work and sharing credit with those who participate in their own.

Top leaders can also take some simple steps to help partners build trusting relationships with one another—for instance, holding retreats that allow them to forge connections. Four months before the annual retreat of Caldwell Partners, a small executive search firm, the CEO asked all partners to name a potential client and to identify a colleague they could work with to try to win that account. At the retreat, the CEO set aside time for people to team up and flesh out their client development approaches. The best firms also pair lateral hires with a successful homegrown partner who's responsible for introducing the newcomer to both other colleagues and clients, thus spreading the coaching function beyond the top executives.

When hiring, leaders need to resist the temptation to bring in high-performing but selfish partners, who might be a toxic influence, and instead seek candidates who have a track record of working across boundaries. To gauge that, ask applicants to give several concrete examples of how they contributed to others' client work and how they built teams to serve their own clients. Candidates who brag about their ability to transfer clients to your firm should send up a red flag. Ask yourself, if clients are so attached to these candidates individually, does that mean that no other professionals at the firm were involved in serving the clients?

Leaders also need to be careful about the signals they send when commending players for great outcomes. If a partner made a big sale but did so as a lone wolf, the leader should not only refrain from celebrating the win but talk with the partner about better ways to achieve the same outcome.

The leader as architect

It might seem commonsensical that if you want people in an organization to behave collaboratively, you should alter the compensation system to reward specific collaborative behaviors. But in both my research and my experience teaching executives, I've repeatedly heard that certain metrics, such as the number of referrals or multipractice pitches, can be gamed, and so trying to reward them is counterproductive.

It's far better to reward the outcomes of effective collaboration, such as rising levels of client satisfaction and client retention, growth in revenue and profits from existing accounts, or the acquisition of new clients in target areas. The annual compensation process at the law firm Duane Morris, for example, involves a "matter contribution analysis," which calculates profitability for individual lawyers by comparing the revenue collected (not just billed) on an attorney's cases with the attorney's costs (including salary and overhead).

To help ensure that these outcomes are achieved in ways consistent with building a collaborative culture, you will need to include measures that capture partners' contributions to nonbillable efforts such as mentoring, sharing knowledge, and giving advice. Management consulting firm A.T. Kearney, for example, assesses its mentor and mentee pairs by having both individuals rate each other's effectiveness using the firm's formal evaluation system.

Leaders can introduce structured ways for professionals to learn enough about others' expertise to identify cross-domain opportunities, credibly discuss them with clients, find trustworthy partners to help carry out the work, and judge their competence. Monthly workshops at practice group meetings that include short presentations from experts in high-potential areas are one approach. Some firms have introduced intranet-based tools for communicating client opportunities, finding experts, and asking or answering questions. Even low-tech options like internal newsletters that feature recent collaborative success stories allow professionals to understand how others in the firm have combined expertise to solve client issues. Results speak for themselves, and so such stories are a powerful way to help professionals gain trust in one another. And a firmwide development and promotion program that links advancement to the demonstration, at a high level, of a range of critical collaboration skills can provide assurance that professionals across the organization have a level of competence that everyone can trust.

To help professionals offer a broader array of services to a client, one leader encouraged high-performing partners to create a "cross-selling SWAT team" that others could draw on for advice. Members of this team accompanied other partners on lunches with clients to help them probe for opportunities, with the understanding that the team members wouldn't fill the openings they helped to unearth.

Beyond this, some firms have introduced a secondment program, in which senior associates or recently promoted partners spend six or 12 months in an overseas office. When they return home, they continue to serve as important links between offices. One firm can typically trace at least three, and sometimes 10 or more, new international referrals between home and host offices in the year following a secondee's return. Some of these referrals go directly to the secondee, but many go to colleagues, with the secondee playing a brokering role. Partners say that they would not have known to contact a partner in the overseas office without that recommendation.

Most professional services firms are already committed to a strategy of growth by seeking out and addressing their clients' most complex problems. And many are finding that those problems can't be addressed by independent specialists—even an army of them. Firms that are landing the highest-value work are focusing more on integrating than on acquiring specialized expertise. They're developing and communicating a strategy that explicitly emphasizes collaboration so that partners understand that their investment in learning to combine forces is part of a broader initiative that the firm will support. In turn, their practice group leaders, who are involved in the development of the overall strategy, are setting clear collaboration objectives for professionals in their departments. Partners who lead client relationship initiatives are being held accountable for identifying multipractice opportunities and making sure they are successfully developed. Under such a deliberately cross-specialty collaboration strategy, time spent learning to work together is treated not as nonbillable overhead but as an investment in remaining competitive. These firms understand that if they can serve the most complex needs of their clients, they will earn their loyalty and the lion's share of the most valuable revenue streams, and leave their competitors to scramble after the increasingly lower-value, commodity work.

Originally published in March 2015. Reprint R1503E

Workspaces That Move People

by Ben Waber, Jennifer Magnolfi, and Greg Lindsay

IN SILICON VALLEY the tight correlation between personal interactions, performance, and innovation is an article of faith, and innovators are building cathedrals reflecting this. Google's new campus is designed to maximize chance encounters. Facebook will soon put several thousand of its employees into a single mile-long room. Yahoo notoriously revoked mobile work privileges because, as the chief of human resources explained, "some of the best decisions and insights come from hallway and cafeteria discussions." And Samsung recently unveiled plans for a new U.S. headquarters, designed in stark contrast to its traditionally hierarchical culture. Vast outdoor areas sandwiched between floors will lure workers into public spaces, where Samsung's executives hope that engineers and salespeople will actually mingle. "The most creative ideas aren't going to come while sitting in front of your monitor," says Scott Birnbaum, a vice president of Samsung Semiconductor. The new building "is really designed to spark not just collaboration but that innovation you see when people collide."

Faith is nice, but do executives have *proof* that this works? Social space like Samsung's could be just another in a long line of fads and broken promises in workspace design: The "action office" becomes the cubicle. Cubicles are torn down for open plans, which leave introverts pining for private space. Quads. Hotel space. Couches. Rotating desk assignments. Standing desks. Treadmill desks. No desks. With apologies to Mark Twain, there's no such thing as a new office design. We just take old ideas, put them into a kind of kaleidoscope, and turn.

How do we know whether any of these approaches is effective? The key metric companies use to measure space—cost per square foot—is focused on efficiency. Few companies measure whether a space's design helps or hurts performance, but they should. They have the means. The same sensors, activity trackers, smartphones, and social networks that they eagerly foist on customers to reveal their habits and behavior can be turned inward, on employees in their work environments, to learn whether it's true that getting engineers and salespeople talking actually works.

Emerging Evidence

We've already begun to collect this kind of performance data using a variety of tools, from simple network analytics to sociometric badges that capture interaction, communication, and location information. After deploying thousands of badges in workplaces ranging from pharmaceuticals, finance, and software companies to hospitals, we've begun to unlock the secrets of good office design in terms of density, proximity of people, and social nature. We've learned, for example, that face-to-face interactions are by far the most important activity in an office. Birnbaum is on to something when he talks about getting employees to "collide," because our data suggest that creating collisions—chance encounters and unplanned interactions between knowledge workers, both inside and outside the organization—improves performance.

We've also learned that spaces can even be designed to produce specific performance outcomes—productivity in one space, say, and increased innovation in another, or both in the same space but at different times. By combining the emerging data with organizational metrics such as total sales or number of new-product launches, we can demonstrate a workspace's effect on the bottom line and then engineer the space to improve it. This will lead to profound changes in how we build our future workspaces. Here are a few.

Idea in Brief

The Challenge

Companies believe that more open space will boost productivity and creativity, but they have no evidence to prove it. They also use cost per square foot as the key metric for managing space.

The Solution

New sensor technology provides data about worker communication and its effect on group performance. It suggests how to design spaces to take advantage of digital work styles and get people bumping into one another, which leads to increased productivity and creativity.

The Future

Designs that encourage "collisions" between digital-savvy workers are being scaled beyond office buildings to improve knowledge worker performance in entire neighborhoods, pointing to a future in which the corporate office is a semipermeable public-private space woven into the urban fabric.

Recognize office space as not just an amortized asset but a strategic tool for growth

The consulting and design firm Strategy Plus estimates that office utilization *peaks* at 42% on any given day. By that logic, the best way to manage cost per square foot is to remove "wasted" square feet. But the data we're generating reveal that investments in re-engineering space for interactions over efficiency can increase sales or new-product launches.

Design offices to reflect how 21st-century digital work actually happens

The buildings we go to every day haven't changed as much as have the tools we use to get work done. Merging digital communication patterns with physical space can increase the probability of interactions that lead to innovation and productivity.

Re-engineer offices to weave a building, a collection of buildings, or a variety of workspaces into the urban fabric

The office of the future will most likely include highly networked, shared, multipurpose spaces that redefine boundaries between companies and improve everyone's performance.

Getting there won't be easy. It will require collecting much more data to inform new design and management principles while engaging urban planners and municipal governments. It will also transform HR, IT, and facilities management from support functions to facilitators. But if companies can change their spaces to reflect how people work, performance improvement will follow. Don't take that on faith. There are data to prove it.

Strategic Coffee Machines

Jon Fredrik Baksaas, the CEO of the Norwegian telecommunications company Telenor, credits the design of the company's Oslo headquarters with helping it shift from a state-run monopoly to a competitive multinational carrier with 150 million subscribers. That design, he says, improved communication, accelerated decision making, and even created what he calls "an attacking mind-set." It was ahead of its time in 2003, when it incorporated "hot desking" (no assigned seats) and spaces that could easily be reconfigured for different tasks and evolving teams.

The design features that make the space effective resulted from a profound shift in mind-set: Baksaas thinks of the offices not as real estate but as a communication tool. Thus strategy, features, and value become more important than cost and efficiency. You'd choose the e-mail provider with the best collaboration and file-transfer features; you can think of space investments the same way.

The improved communication Telenor achieved in its new space can be explained by Alex "Sandy" Pentland's April 2012 HBR article, "The New Science of Building Great Teams." Pentland deployed badges (the same kind now used by Ben Waber's firm) that track how people talk to one another, who talks with whom, how people move around the office, and where they spend time. (Devices were worn on an opt-in basis, and individual data were anonymous and unavailable to employers.) Pentland identified three key elements of successful communication: *exploration* (interacting with people in many other social groups), *engagement* (interacting with people within your social group, in reasonably equal doses), and *energy* (interacting with more people overall).

Spaces designed to promote these activities increase the likelihood of collisions—and the data repeatedly demonstrate that more collisions create positive outcomes. We don't measure the content of interactions, but that doesn't matter. When collisions occur, regardless of their content, improvement typically follows.

Spaces can be designed to favor exploration or engagement or energy to achieve certain outcomes. For example, if a call center wants improved productivity, the space should favor engagement—getting the team to interact more. Higher engagement is typically accomplished not with open social space but with tight, walled-off workstations and adjacent spaces for small-group collaboration and interaction. The team's break area becomes a crucial collision space. At one call center, the company expanded the break room and gave reps more time to hang out there with colleagues. Paradoxically, productivity shot up after the change. Away from their phones, the reps could circulate knowledge within the group.

Then again, for a company that—like Telenor—is trying to innovate or change, increasing engagement can be detrimental, because it takes time away from crucial exploration with other groups and outsiders. Telenor's open, public, and flexible space values exploration much more than engagement—it begs employees to meet in the open, where they may bump into unexpected people, and allows them to claim spaces and shape them for brainstorming sessions.

Once a company has identified the pattern it's trying to achieve and how the pattern affects outcomes, it can begin to calculate the value of workspaces, not just their costs. For example, we deployed sociometric badges with about 50 executives at a pharmaceuticals company who were responsible for nearly $1 billion in annual sales. They wanted to increase sales but didn't know what behaviors would help. Even if sales went up, they couldn't necessarily say why.

The data collected over some weeks showed that when a salesperson increased interactions with coworkers on other teams—that is, increased exploration—by 10%, his or her sales also grew by 10%. An elegant correlation.

So the executives asked, How can we change our space to get the sales staff running into colleagues from other departments? In this case, the answer lay with coffee. At the time, the company had roughly one coffee machine for every six employees, and the same people used the same machines every day. The sales force commiserated with itself. Marketing people talked to marketing people.

The company invested several hundred thousand dollars to rip out the coffee stations and build fewer, bigger ones—just one for every 120 employees. It also created a large cafeteria for all employees in place of a much smaller one that few employees had used. In the quarter after the coffee-and-cafeteria switch, sales rose by 20%, or $200 million, quickly justifying the capital investment in the redesign.

Managers might be tempted to simply build big social spaces and expect great results, but it's not that simple. Companies must have an understanding of what they're trying to achieve (higher productivity? more creativity?) before changing a space. For example, what worked at the pharma company didn't work at a large furniture manufacturer that transformed its headquarters from classic cubicles to an open-plan office in which approximately 60% of the workforce had unassigned seating. To test the plan, we deployed badges with 65 sales and marketing team members on a single floor before and after the reconfiguration.

The call center's goal was to get the members of one team talking to improve productivity. Telenor and the pharma company needed space that encouraged people to collide with *other* groups. The furniture company's success required something in between: tight integration across the sales cycle, which meant some exploration and then high engagement among specific groups that needed to communicate more.

The company had hypothesized that fewer desks and a smaller footprint would move people closer together, increasing the likelihood of interaction. Unassigned seating would make interaction between people in different groups more likely. Such interaction did increase, by 17%—but energy levels (the number of individuals' encounters during the day) dropped by an average of 14%. This suggests that the space simply reshuffled stationary workers rather than creating movement. Someone from marketing might bump into new people because their temporary desks happened to be close by, but

A beginner's guide to space design

If you want to reconfigure your office space to improve performance, this simple grid will help you get started. It uses two important factors in office design—relative openness and seating flexibility—to suggest what configuration will lead to one of four distinct outcomes.

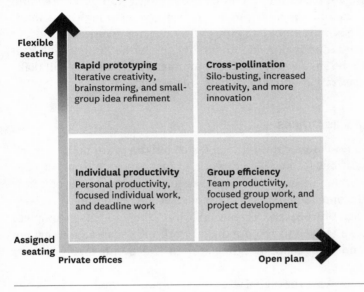

none of them were leaving their workstations once they got there. As a result, team communication dropped by 45%. The company saved money on space by reducing the number of fixed workstations, but both revenue and productivity plummeted.

The type of interaction that's most valuable changes according to goals; what doesn't change is that interaction in itself is far more valuable than we realize. Sometimes circulating, exploring, engaging, and increasing the number of people's collisions is more important than individual productivity or creativity. Imagine, for example, that a worker finds a better way to do her job but never tells anyone else doing the same job what she discovered. She has improved her performance but no one else's. If she takes time out of her day to tell others about what she's learned, her productivity drops—but she has increased theirs. We've shown that in some cases even a 5% drop in personal productivity can have a positive outcome on group performance.

Think of the implications: First, most employee performance reviews are based on individual productivity and don't take into consideration how group productivity can grow through more interaction. Second, untold amounts of money are invested in tools to increase individual productivity, but the money might be better used to design a workplace that promotes collisions that will make the organization—not individuals—more successful.

Lobbies as Offices

One factor complicates all this: Office buildings are no longer the sole locations for knowledge work. In fact, research from the consulting group Emergent Research suggests that two-thirds of it now happens outside the office. Consequently, no matter how precisely we design office space to create collisions, the design is incomplete if it doesn't take into account digital work and collaboration that are independent of space and time and for which immediacy is more important.

In some ways the digital workspace enhances in-person collisions with file-sharing and communication tools such as chat, e-mail, and archiving. It can gather more ideas from more places: Research indicates that interactions and engagement decrease as the physical distance between work groups gets bigger, whereas online engagement increases with the number of users. However, data show that digital communication can't replace face-to-face interaction and may actually be enhanced by it (see the sidebar "The Allen Curve Holds"). Studies with sociometric badges confirm that remote teams don't perform as well as those in physical proximity.

Furthermore, the upgrade cycles of buildings and technology don't mesh. Telenor's state-of-the-art campus, which smartly integrated digital features such as a wireless file-sharing system—was built four years before the iPhone was introduced and before Wi-Fi

The Allen Curve Holds

IN HIS SEMINAL 1977 BOOK, *Managing the Flow of Technology,* Thomas J. Allen was the first to measure the strong negative correlation between physical distance and frequency of communication. The "Allen curve" estimates that we are four times as likely to communicate regularly with someone sitting six feet away from us as with someone 60 feet away, and that we almost never communicate with colleagues on separate floors or in separate buildings.

But the office is no longer just a physical place; we can enter it by logging on, attend meetings from anywhere, and collaborate on documents without ever seeing one another. It would seem that distance-shrinking technologies break the Allen curve, and that communication no longer correlates to distance.

Wrong. The Allen curve holds. In fact, as distance-shrinking technology accelerates, proximity is apparently becoming more important. Studies by Ben Waber show that both face-to-face and digital communications follow the Allen curve. In one study, engineers who shared a physical office were 20% more likely to stay in touch digitally than those who worked elsewhere. When they needed to collaborate closely, co-located coworkers e-mailed four times as frequently as colleagues in different locations, which led to 32% faster project completion times.

Out of sight, out of sync.

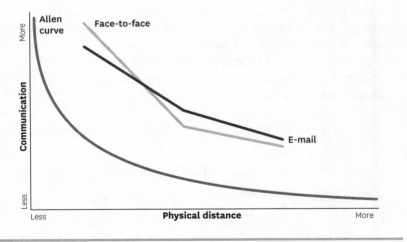

became ubiquitous. Just a few years later, Telenor's then-novel proprietary wireless network would have been designed radically differently—if its features weren't obviated by cloud storage and other developments. All of which is to say that understanding how digital and physical spaces work together is crucial to improving workspace but also an incredibly complicated design challenge.

Workers themselves have been the first to take on this challenge. Just as IT has been consumerized over the past decade, digital-savvy employees are beginning to demand that their spaces adapt to how they work, rather than vice versa. This shift began in earnest in 2005, in San Francisco, London, and Berlin. Technologists, programmers, and creative professionals wanted to work outside confining office environments but also to avoid the isolation of home offices. They chose to work side by side, in what are known as coworking spaces.

Early examples were organic, built by users rather than by design professionals. They were accessible to anyone and sometimes free. People who chose to work in those spaces intentionally sought members from different organizations, thus reproducing the community, social interaction, learning, and energy typical of their online work, while adding the benefit of physical proximity to others. Unwittingly, they were engineering spaces to create the exploration that we know enhances creativity. And it worked. Studying 45 coworking spaces around the world, one of us, Jennifer Magnolfi, discovered that people had chosen them because they believed that their performance would improve more rapidly in such spaces than in an office building or at home. A 2011 *Deskmag* survey of more than 1,500 coworkers in 52 countries supported her findings:

- 75% reported an increase in productivity since joining their space

- 80% reported an increase in the size of their business network

- 92% reported an increase in the size of their social circle

- 86% reported a decrease in their sense of isolation

- 83% reported that they trusted others in their coworking space

By 2013, according to data from Emergent Research, more than 160,000 people were using several thousand coworking spaces in the United States and Europe. The organization forecasts that in five years more than one million people will be using 12,000 coworking spaces globally. Another survey showed that by 2014, 72% of participants were forecasting an increase in their income.

The growth of coworking and surveys of coworkers demonstrate that given the choice, people will choose workspaces that support their digital style while giving them access to new knowledge, exposing them to different kinds of expertise, and accelerating their learning. Coworking's success has helped some teams "graduate" out of their coworking spaces. Although the model clearly provides the exploration that independent workers and very small groups need, when teams reach a critical size, usually around 10 members, they need to up their engagement with one another. Private office space and conference rooms become necessary parts of their workday.

This has led to the scaling of coworking space. What started as small spaces for a few independent workers grew into start-up accelerators—groups of start-ups sharing some of the private collaboration space available to them. Eventually large corporations mimicked the idea by creating shared space where their employees could work with partners, researchers, and customers. The first floor of Amazon's new campus in Seattle is mostly coworking space. Ace Hotel actively markets the lobby of its New York flagship as a workspace. AT&T has created Foundry, a network of research centers in which its engineers work side by side with handpicked start-ups, corporate partners, and third-party developers to bring new products to market faster. Even bankers are doing it: ING Direct built seven cafés (now called Capital One 360 Cafés) where its workers could set up shop and interact with customers who could also use the space for work. Perhaps less surprisingly, and true to form, Airbnb has made one of the conference rooms at its new headquarters bookable (through Airbnb, of course) by anyone in San Francisco, free.

What's Happening in Vegas

Coworking is succeeding because it successfully integrates good workspace design that enhances exploration with the digital work habits of individuals and small teams. In some cases it's possible to scale the benefits of coworking—such as high collision rates and accelerated learning—to build an entire neighborhood.

The Downtown Project, in Las Vegas, is an early example of the concept. Tony Hsieh, the CEO of Zappos, is investing $350 million in the area around the company's new headquarters, which is the former city hall. Hsieh's goal is to grow the local start-up and entrepreneurial community in a way that will organically attract talent to the area, benefiting both Zappos employees and the neighborhood.

Jennifer Magnolfi participated in the development and analysis of coworking space inside Zappos headquarters and led a local coworking experiment that launched in early 2012 and eventually grew to include nearly 200 stakeholders, among them Zappos employees, area residents, start-ups, independent workers, and others. The spaces were improvised from a network of existing ones: a coffee shop, the courtyard of a Thai restaurant, an old church hall, the lobby of a casino, and an empty corporate apartment.

Early results show that the small, shared nature of the neighborhood fostered mobility that created collisions on a greater scale. Exploration and energy were very high. After six months, data revealed a 42% increase in face-to-face encounters, a 78% increase in participant-generated proposals to solve specific problems, and an 84% increase in the number of new leaders—participants who initiated work and collaboration and developed project scope and objectives. Ten new civic and local community projects were launched—including the Sunday Reset Project, a monthly event to promote healthful living.

Zappos and the Downtown Project have continued experimenting with the area and are using a new metric: "collisionable hours," or the number of probable interactions per hour per acre. Hsieh's goal is to reach 100,000 collisionable hours per acre in the neighborhood—about 2.3 per square foot per year.

The Downtown Project is still a controlled experiment. It doesn't capture the complexity of getting companies and civic entities to cooperate, routinely and continually, while also adapting to inevitable technological change. Nor does it address the complexity of getting a multinational to integrate coworking space when it's already managing a global office portfolio. (See the sidebar "What About the Global Company?") But it points to a new model for the corporate

What About the Global Company?

WHAT HAPPENS when proximity isn't feasible? When our colleagues are not only in different buildings but in different countries? One consumer packaged goods company we know of is trying to address these questions. It has a global real estate portfolio of more than 200 million square feet supporting 300,000 employees in 26 countries. Managing for collisions at this scale requires a two-pronged approach. First, like Telenor, the company must treat the buildings as communication tools, using more open environments and denser workspaces to promote interactions.

Second, it must link those optimized buildings in a virtual space that makes communication between them as easy and effective as possible. To achieve that, it has created a "community manager" role for workspace operations, bridging facilities management, technology, and corporate communications. The role is modeled on those found in online communities such as Yelp and Airbnb and in coworking spaces. The company's community manager tries to create virtual collisions by making it easy for people who can't interact in person to connect through online and social channels.

campus of the future that weaves together public and private spaces, employees and partners, living and working. Hsieh and others believe that companies designed on this model will be more productive and innovative—as businesses and as communities—and in the long term will gain a strategic advantage over companies that cut off their employees from the exploration that improves performance.

———————

More than a century ago, Frederick Winslow Taylor brought his stopwatch and principles of scientific management to the office, instilling efficiency as the highest calling in what was then a factory for processing paperwork. Today we have the means to measure the performance of modern idea factories. Even these early insights suggest a future in which we must aggressively change the definition of what workspace is, from *where* work is done to *how* it's done, and then design spaces—physical and digital—around that. The office of the past was a literal box of cubicles and desks, meeting rooms and common spaces. In the office of the future, we'll be thinking and working outside it.

Originally published in October 2014. Reprint R1410E

Digital Ubiquity

How Connections, Sensors, and Data Are Revolutionizing Business. *by Marco Iansiti and Karim R. Lakhani*

FOR MORE THAN A CENTURY General Electric made most of its revenue by selling industrial hardware and repair services. But in recent years GE was at increasing risk of losing many of its top customers to nontraditional competitors—IBM and SAP on the one hand, and big-data start-ups on the other. Those competitors aimed to shift the customer value proposition away from acquiring reliable industrial equipment to deriving new efficiencies and other benefits through advanced analytics and algorithms based on the data generated by that equipment. The trend threatened to turn GE into a commodity equipment provider.

In 2011 GE responded with a multibillion-dollar initiative focused on what it calls the industrial internet. The company is adding digital sensors to its machines, connecting them to a common, cloud-based software platform, investing in modern software development capabilities, building advanced analytics capabilities, and embracing crowdsourced product development. All this is transforming the company's business model. Now revenue from its jet engines, for example, is tied not to a simple sales transaction but to performance improvements: less downtime and more miles flown over the course of a year. Such digitally enabled, outcomes-based approaches helped GE generate more than $1.5 billion in incremental income in 2013; the company expects that number to double in 2014 and again in 2015.

GE's industrial internet is based on the newfound ubiquity of digital connectivity. Most information work is already digitized through the use of connected laptops and mobile devices. Now, with the growth of the "internet of things," the pervasive deployment of digital sensors is extending digitization and connectivity to previously analog tasks, processes, and machine and service operations. Moreover, virtually limitless computing power is available at very low cost through cloud computing. The combined impact of all this is that both established and start-up players in every industry are being forced to compete in new ways. (See the sidebar "What Makes Digital Technology Transformational?")

Digital ubiquity started with the transformation of software companies. For example, Microsoft and SAP, which used to make large profits by selling software licenses, are investing heavily in infrastructure to support cloud software and analytics; switching from product to service revenue; and experimenting with outcomes-based business models in cases where revenue might be tied to the efficiencies delivered by an enterprise application. Joining them are newer players such as Salesforce, Workday, Google, and Amazon Web Services, whose cloud-native services are already transforming enterprise software. But the trend reaches well beyond software companies: The medical device maker Becton Dickinson is investing heavily in software and development capabilities that will incorporate increased connectivity, intelligence, and platform functionality in its diagnostics equipment. Companies in the investment management sector, such as Wealthfront and AltX, are assembling data platforms that optimize and automate the investing process. Even Domino's, the pizza company, is building digital capabilities, mobile technologies, and analytics to enhance innovation and meet consumer expectations regarding service, transparency, and speedy delivery.

Adapting to ubiquitous digital connectivity is now essential to competitiveness in most sectors of our economy. We have examined transformation across dozens of industries and companies—both traditional and born-digital. We have talked to hundreds of executives in our effort to understand how traditional modes of innovation

Idea in Brief

The Finding

Digital transformation—the digitization of previously analog machine and service operations, organizational tasks, and managerial processes—is pushing both established and start-up players in many industries to compete in new ways.

The Implication

To compete, companies will have to rethink their business models,

identifying new opportunities for creating and capturing value.

The Example

General Electric has invested millions in its "industrial internet," linking previously discrete tasks and equipment to create more than $1.5 billion in incremental revenue in 2013—an amount it expects will double in 2014 and again in 2015.

and operational execution are changing. (Disclosure: We have consulted with or have interests in several of the companies mentioned in this article.) We have seen that digital transformation is no traditional disruption scenario: The paradigm is not displacement and replacement but connectivity and recombination. Transactions are being digitized, data is being generated and analyzed in new ways, and previously discrete objects, people, and activities are being connected (see the exhibit "An explosion in connected devices"). Incumbents can use their existing assets, dramatically increase their value, and defend against (or partner with) entrants. Pacific Gas and Electric, for example, will be more valuable if it connects with Nest, the digital thermostat that Google recently bought for $3.2 billion. (See the sidebar "Why Nest Matters.") And Uber makes money by bringing drivers together with customers—not by replacing them.

Rethinking Value Creation and Capture

A business model is defined by two things: how the organization creates value for its customers (the customer value proposition) and how it captures that value (how it makes money). Digital transformation changes both.

What Makes Digital Technology Transformational?

TO UNDERSTAND WHY the internet of things is transforming business models, it's helpful to understand three fundamental properties of digital technology: (1) Unlike analog signals, digital signals can be transmitted perfectly, without error. A Facebook webpage will look exactly the same when it's generated in Palo Alto as it does when it's shown to a consumer in Bangalore. (2) Moreover, digital signals can be replicated indefinitely—that same page can be shown to a billion Facebook users—without any degradation. (3) Once the investment in network infrastructure has been made, the page can be communicated to the incremental consumer at zero (or almost zero) marginal cost. And a digital task performed at zero marginal cost will immediately supersede any traditional analog task completed at significant marginal cost (which is why e-mail and social networks are killing "snail mail").

These properties (exact replication infinite times at zero marginal cost) improve the scalability of operations and make it easy to combine new and old business processes and connect industries and communities to generate novel opportunities. Facebook can connect any brand to any user community without incremental expense. A sensor on a GE jet engine can transmit useful data predicting maintenance over long distances at zero incremental cost; this data can in turn be communicated to GE's maintenance organization and third-party spare parts manufacturers. Thus these three fundamental properties drive the transformation enabled by ubiquitous digital technology.

Consider GE's wind farm deal with the global energy giant E.ON. In the past, as the demand for power increased, GE would try to sell more turbines and associated equipment to power-generation companies. In its partnership with E.ON, GE used E.ON's extensive operational data to run advanced analytics and simulations and come up with a different scenario: Instead of increasing capacity by adding more wind turbine hardware, E.ON could meet demand with a relatively modest purchase of equipment to connect all the turbines through software that allows for dynamic control and real-time analytics.

GE creates value by extracting useful data from the sensors on its turbines and other wind energy equipment and using that information to optimize equipment performance, utilization, and maintenance. It captures that value by charging a percentage of the

An explosion in connected devices

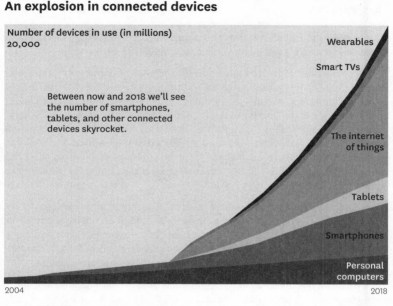

Number of devices in use (in millions)
20,000

Wearables

Smart TVs

Between now and 2018 we'll see the number of smartphones, tablets, and other connected devices skyrocket.

The internet of things

Tablets

Smartphones

Personal computers

2004

2018

Source: BI intelligence estimates based on data from Gartner Research, IDC, Strategy Analytics, Machina Research, and others

customer's incremental revenue from improved performance. So although GE sells less hardware, it has developed a mutually profitable long-term partnership.

GE's Transformation

When Jeffrey Immelt became GE's CEO, in 2001, he inherited a company that was efficient but facing intense competition and falling prices for its top-tier capital goods. Immelt accelerated the company's movement toward contract service agreements (CSAs), instituted under his predecessor, Jack Welch. CSAs guaranteed total operational management of an asset, including preventive maintenance and repairs. They generated reliable high-margin income for GE over the life of the equipment—often several decades. By 2005

Why Nest Matters

A YEAR AGO few Honeywell executives saw Google as a competitor. That changed in January 2014, when Google bought Nest, the digital thermostat and smoke detector company, for $3.2 billion. The move is a clear indication that digital transformation and connection are reaching critical mass, spreading across even the most traditional industrial segments.

The Nest thermostat creates value by digitizing the entire home-temperature-control process—from fuel purchase to temperature setting to powering the heating, ventilation, and air-conditioning system—and connecting it to Nest's cloud data services. The thermostat aggregates its data on real-time energy consumption and shares that data with utilities, which can improve their energy consumption forecasts and thus achieve greater efficiency. And Nest can push cost data back to customers ("Current demand is high, so the price you pay is going up. We will turn down your air conditioning for the next two hours"), reducing their energy bills.

How does Nest capture the value it creates? First, its retail prices are double or triple those of conventional thermostats. Second, it can make money from electric utilities on the basis of outcomes: Google can aggregate data on energy-consumption patterns and offer the utilities a service in return for a percentage of their savings. Third, it can pass some of those savings back to consumers.

Thus Nest will not only play in the $3 billion global thermostat industry; it will help shape the $6 trillion energy sector. It can also jump into other sectors by opening up its digital cloud platform to devices and services from other providers. For example, the platform now connects with advanced Whirlpool laundry systems to schedule wash and dry cycles during nonpeak hours. It works with the wearable-technology company Jawbone to detect when someone has awakened and then dynamically adjust the home temperature. It can connect with home security ("Someone just walked by your thermostat; I thought no one was home") and consumer electronics ("Since you're now in the bedroom, do you really want to keep the TV on in the den?"). The potential for new applications and services is astonishing.

CSAs accounted for more than 75% of GE's revenue backlog and contributed the same proportion to industrial earnings.

"We have globalized the company while investing massive amounts in technology, products, and services," Immelt told an industry group in 2009. "We know we must change again." That change was the industrial internet. GE's initiative proposes an open global network of machines, data, and people to generate a plethora

The evolution of GE service models

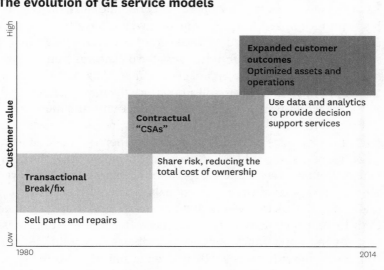

of new business opportunities and outcomes-based business models. It focuses on providing data synthesis and analysis and designing real-time and predictive solutions to optimize the complex operations of its customers.

The industrial internet is revolutionizing value creation and capture for GE. The decision to build out the new system was more evolutionary. By 2011, along with sensors and microprocessors, GE had significant embedded software running power plants, jet engines, hospitals and medical systems, utility companies, oil rigs, rail, and other industrial infrastructure worldwide. Connecting the hundreds of thousands of GE devices to one another and arming them with increasingly sophisticated sensors seemed like a logical extension of the maintenance-and-operations-driven business model, and one that would extend GE's strategic advantages. "I have a great deal of confidence in our core hardware," Immelt says. "We have the most stuff. It's hard to replicate. We started from a real position of relative strength."

Building software capabilities

As the scale and scope of the opportunity became clear, Immelt and his team recognized that the company would have to build new capabilities. It would need a global center to develop and support software applications uniformly across the businesses, and it would need new and innovative approaches to managing customer relationships—including how to sell and service the new offerings.

GE is a world-beater in efficiency, productivity, and innovation. But it had never been known for the agility, responsiveness, and strategic coherence of its software development process. Indeed, when Immelt launched GE Software, in November 2011, the company's IT efforts were scattered. Its various business units employed more than 12,000 software professionals, who helped generate several billion dollars in revenue. But no overarching strategy guided their technical choices and commercial offerings. Each business unit—even each product leader—made choices according to local conditions; the result was wildly uneven technical and commercial performance. "Every one of our products had a different underpinning platform, architecture, technology, and set of vendors," says William Ruh, whom Immelt brought in from Cisco to run the new operation. Ruh and other GE senior leaders set out to get a handle on the scope of the company's existing software operations globally; they found 136 products, of which only 17 were actually profitable. "It was taking us years to build the software, and years to get it out the door," Ruh says. "And customers' needs were changing too rapidly to keep up."

Developer talent was also a concern. "Our software engineers had experience in one of two ways," Ruh says. "They were either mechanical engineers or they were computer scientists. But most of them had experience with technologies that were last-generation. They were very reliant on outside vendors, sometimes for full development." Furthermore, GE's software specialists were spread across the global businesses and had no common language. Ruh started assembling his own team and insisted that its members all work together at GE Software headquarters, in San Ramon, California. "Co-location is everything," he says. "New things are easier to create a team around when they are all in one place." By January 2013 Ruh had hired 62 people; that June about 150 employees moved into the new offices. At the end of the year the team numbered 350, only 2% of whom had transferred from other parts of the company. Ruh expects to have more than 1,000 software developers and data scientists working at the San Ramon facility by the end of 2014.

Ruh set out to create a software platform that would work across the entire enterprise. It would make developing new applications more efficient and allow for rapid cross-industry innovation. It would also enable independent developers to build applications on GE's platform. And Ruh insisted that GE own all the intellectual property his team built.

The team rolled out its first set of solutions under the Predictivity brand, running on Predix, GE's common software platform. Predix and Predictivity promise to dramatically streamline monitoring and maintenance for all GE's industrial technologies. Predix combines distributed computing and big-data analytics, asset management, machine-to-machine communication, security, and mobility. Predictivity will eventually connect all GE's machines to the cloud (no small feat, given that some business units, such as health care, have thousands of products, each with its own complex software needs and legacy systems), enabling them to talk to one another, learn from historical data, and provide predictive information to help eliminate unplanned downtime and otherwise improve efficiency.

Public Service Enterprise Group (PSEG), a New York– and New Jersey–based utility, is using a Predictivity product to react to real-time changes in power demand, grid conditions, and fuel supply. In the few months that the asset-optimization solution has been in place, PSEG has increased output by 6%, reduced fuel burn by more than 1.5%, and increased operational flexibility for its gas turbine fleet. St. Luke's Medical Center, in Phoenix, uses another Predictivity solution to integrate bed assignments, departmental workflow, patient flow, transportation, and equipment management, reducing bed-turnaround times by 51 minutes—a critical factor in hospital capacity planning and patient satisfaction. And a railroad customer, Norfolk Southern, uses a Predictivity network-optimization solution to move more freight faster and more intelligently, achieving a 10% increase in the overall speed of trains, a 50% reduction in losses due to "expired crews" (personnel who have to meet time-off require-ments), and significant on-time performance improvements.

Getting business-unit buy-in for GE Software was often a chal-lenge. The business units were accustomed to operating autono-mously, and some were more legacy-laden than others. Ruh did not try to force anyone to comply. "I said, 'We're going to do this; you can be on the train or not,'" he recalls. "A number wanted to, so we developed them at a very fast pace and got them successful quickly. The performance gains and revenue enhancements were visible to other executives, who then asked their own businesses, 'If you're not doing this, why not?' And there was no good answer." Before long all the business units were working with the initiative.

It helped that Ruh's division was structured to encourage collabo-ration. Funded by the CEO's office, GE Software does not have its own P&L. "I don't compete with the businesses," Ruh says. "I don't get confused by trying to build my business versus theirs. I'm tied to and care about their P&L because I'm aligned with the question 'Did we have business impact?'"

While Ruh and his team pushed forward on the common plat-form, Immelt and Beth Comstock, GE's chief marketing officer, con-sidered the new offerings' implications for the marketing and sales teams. From the outset some managers argued that selling analyt-ics and other software offerings was beyond GE's scope, whereas others argued that licensing the offerings was a cleaner model and therefore preferable. The challenge is that "we're trying to sell them something they don't know they need," as Comstock puts it. "And they can't see when it works."

Learning to sell the new model

GE had to make a dramatic shift in approach. It had to abandon its traditional "box seller" mentality in favor of solution-based sales that focused not only on pain points but also on exactly how to enhance the customer's operating performance. "The transition we have to make with our customers is going from agreements that

What SmartWool Learned from Its Digital Customers

UBIQUITOUS CONNECTIVITY can reshape marketing and product in-novation. Digital networks, for example, can *leverage user data* and *drive efficiency* in advertising and lead generation. They can also connect man-ufacturers directly to communities of product users and "fans"—making it possible to crowdsource innovative ideas with ease.

When executives at SmartWool, a maker of high-performance athletic apparel, wanted to reach their core customers with a new ad campaign, they went to Victors & Spoils, an open digital advertising company. The V&S team quickly discovered that the last thing SmartWool's loyal customers wanted was more traditional advertising; instead these outdoorsy types were eager to participate more meaningfully with the company.

In thinking about product design and marketing, SmartWool had always looked to world-class athletes for guidance—an old-school approach based on the view that expert knowledge was scarce. V&S flipped the paradigm and, through Facebook, recruited a community to test SmartWool's products. Six months after the launch of the campaign, SmartWool had signed up 2,500 field testers—more than 10% of its Facebook following. These enthusiastic fans bought the new products and put them to rigorous use right away. But the real bonanza for SmartWool was that the testers flooded the company with novel insights about the products' performance, suggested improve-ments, and offered ideas for new products. For example, fans requested that SmartWool add thumbholes to its jacket sleeves so that they could function as mittens. They also wanted lighter-weight running socks in a broader selec-tion of colors. The company's designers accommodated them.

The whole process culminated in an advertising campaign. V&S incorporated SmartWool's new embrace of its crowd in ads featuring its field testers and their innovations. The campaign has performed well online and in print, improving both brand message retention and e-commerce conversion. Ex-ecutives at V&S and SmartWool say they were surprised by the customers' passion and acknowledge that they could never have tapped into it without the digital connection. Now that SmartWool has opened the channel to fans, it's finding new ways to bring them into every part of the product innovation and marketing development processes.

are break/fix to agreements that guarantee outcomes," Immelt says. "Those will happen customer by customer, and the outcome guarantees are going to cannibalize the break/fix."

GE is now rethinking and redeveloping its go-to-market and commercialization strategies. To help evolve its sales organization, Immelt brought in Kate Johnson as chief commercial officer, a new position within the marketing function. Johnson had deep experience in selling and servicing enterprise software at Red Hat and Oracle; she worked to create and expand GE's outcomes-based sales capabilities. She also oversaw a new commercial center of excellence that crystallized how GE would increase service revenue and margin growth. "This change is not just about sales," Johnson says. "It's about product management, marketing, sales and commercial operations, delivery. It involves the whole life cycle, from invention to fulfillment. And that is the essence of how we're tackling the problem."

To be sure, GE still needs salespeople and account executives who have deep relationships with their clients. However, what they sell, how they sell, and to whom they sell is changing completely. The sales team now includes solution architects, who combine exhaustive industrial knowledge with advanced analytics to develop models for setting and achieving business outcomes. "Instead of a features list with pricing and discount caps," Johnson says, "we're shaping deals from the ground up that are based on the value derived by the customer. It's a completely different set of economics that is very disruptive in the industry."

Customer engagement has become far more complex. It requires an approach to solution development that integrates technology, connectivity, and analytics products from GE with the client's proprietary financial and operational data. "For this kind of sale, we need much more data to truly understand our customers' business and financial situation, how they make money," Johnson says. "Our sales team now has to do a whole range of new spreadsheet calculations and modeling before we even approach a potential customer."

For example, the E.ON contract started off with GE's proposing two capital-expenditure deals and one operational-expenditure deal to improve energy performance on E.ON's wind farms. Structuring the three options required extensive familiarity with the client's balance sheet, financial strategies, and approach to the market. The GE sales team had to manage E.ON's procurement and accounting officers and also had to work closely with its technologists to address concerns about measuring performance. It developed a complete methodology, shared it through white papers, and piloted the technology on selected E.ON turbines. The deal itself required layers of agreement within the client, from purchasing to asset management to finance and operations. In the end, the operational-expenditure model won out. E.ON accepted the assessments and methodology and was pleased that very little capital had to be spent to capture gains.

Building out the ecosystem

Immelt, Ruh, and Comstock were aware that they could go only so far in developing offerings. They needed to strengthen the loose network of suppliers, distributors, and developers of related products and services that enable and enhance GE's offerings. It's an approach that technology companies such as Apple and Microsoft have benefited from for years, as have Walmart and other highly tech-dependent businesses.

The challenge was especially tricky for GE. Each of GE's industry sectors was at a different stage of maturity, and each business unit had its own legacy software issues that constrained product innovation. "We have to face the limitations on the ecosystem," Immelt says. "We started from the idea of asset optimization and no unplanned downtime, but in the end, the maximum customer value is going to be in the ecosystem. How open do we want this to be? How far are we willing to go?"

To build out its ecosystem, GE is experimenting with different types of partnerships. Joint ventures, for example, let a smaller concern run with a discrete idea, keeping it free of GE's internal pressures. Caradigm, a 50/50 joint venture formed by GE Healthcare and Microsoft in February 2012, developed software to enable health systems and payers to drive continuous improvement in care. Taleris, a joint venture between GE Aviation and Accenture that developed software and analytics capabilities to manage airline operations, recently signed its first multibillion-dollar deal with Etihad Airways, of the United Arab Emirates, to predict maintenance issues and recommend preventive approaches.

GE is also relying more on crowdsourcing for innovation. The company has invested in Quirky, a consumer product innovation platform and manufacturer with more than 744,000 members, to propose, refine, select, fund, and build new products, and has offered its relationships with suppliers and other support for products as they launch. The investment helped get four products—a smartphone-enabled power strip, a physical dashboard that displays online information, a smart egg tray (which connects with your mobile device to tell you how many eggs you have and how fresh they are), and a multifunction sensor (motion/sound/light/temperature/humidity) for home use—onto the shelves at Home Depot and Best Buy before the 2013 holiday season. More recently GE announced a smartphone-powered window air conditioner for the home market.

GE Aviation partnered with Alaska Airlines in November 2012 to present Flight Quest, making two months' worth of FlightStats data available on an open platform. Outsiders were challenged to come up with algorithms that could better predict flight arrival times, with a total of $250,000 awarded to the top five entries. The winner, a doctor in Switzerland, developed an algorithm that predicted arrival times 40% more accurately than the existing technology. More recently, Local Motors, an Arizona-based company that has crowdsourced vehicle design since 2007, partnered with GE to debut a manufacturing process and increase by an order of magnitude the number of products designed and market-tested in the appliances division.

GE has also partnered with potential competitors, including Intel for sensor technology, Cisco for network hardware, Accenture for service delivery, and Amazon Web Services for cloud delivery. As Ruh notes, "One big fear when partnering with companies like these is the competitive risks." Immelt says, "We partner with competitors. We know there's going to be tons of things we learn and share or give away. You can say on the outside, 'You are opening up Pandora's box. You're going to lose some of the control you have today.' I think that's part of the debate."

The tremendous opportunities created by GE's digital transformation don't come risk-free. As the company continues on this path, it will need to keep building software capabilities and defining software strategies that capture value without alienating participants in the ecosystem. The choices it makes about the openness of its platform will be crucial. Moreover, GE's business model will be increasingly tied to those of its customers.

Beyond GE

GE is just one of many companies being completely reshaped by the new ubiquity of digital technology. Microsoft's CEO, Satya Nadella, is trying to move his company past reliance on sales of its packaged software to remake it as a provider of cloud-enabled productivity services that operate on any platform or device. Microsoft's transformation will recombine and restructure every one of its products and businesses. And as core applications such as Outlook and Office rapidly turn toward service-based business models (Outlook.com and Office 365), Nadella and his team are looking at new monetization approaches. Revenue from packaged software is giving way to value capture based on customer usage.

Like GE, Ford is working in a variety of partnerships to create information-based offerings and is structuring new relationships with major Silicon Valley players. CEO Mark Fields is investing in the development of new business models: Ford and Zipcar have experimented with car-sharing on U.S. college campuses, and Ford is piloting a Zipcar-like program in Germany. In cooperation with other start-ups, Ford is working on services such as enabling drivers to reserve parking spaces and enforcing residential parking rules. And it is looking to create on-demand ride-sharing. Meanwhile, Daimler has established a car-sharing service, car2go, that operates in 26 cities in Europe and North America, and it recently acquired RideScout, an Uber rival that operates in 69 cities in North America.

Bank of America is investing in its relationship with the investment platform Wealthfront, bringing analytics and automation to consumer portfolio investing. The bank is now using Wealthfront's services to manage more than $1 billion in investments, rather than relying on its traditional portfolio choice and optimization processes. In the hedge fund arena, ValueAct is working with iMatchative to create integrated data platforms—from fund performance to novel investor and fund-manager psychometrics—and more-streamlined, digitized decision processes. The list goes on.

Approaching Digital Ubiquity

Over time, digital technology and the internet of things will transform virtually every sector and every business. Here's how you can embrace them, using lessons from the companies we studied.

Apply the digital lens to existing products and services

We still live in an analog world. However, over the next five years many business components will be digitized to enable a new range of products, services, and business models. Consider how Uber has transformed transportation services by digitizing all aspects of reservations, tracking, billing, customer service, driver performance, and ratings. What cumbersome processes in your business or industry are amenable to instrumentation and connectivity? Which ones are most challenging to you or your customers?

Connect your existing assets across companies

If you work in a traditional analog setting, examine your assets for new opportunities and look at other industries and the start-up world for new synergies. Your customer connections are especially valuable, as are your knowledge of customers' needs and the capabilities you built to meet them. Nest is connecting with public utilities to share data and optimize overall energy usage. If you work in a start-up, don't just focus on driving the obsolescence of established companies. Look at how you can connect with and enhance their value and extract some of it for yourself.

Examine new modes of value creation

What new data could you accumulate, and where could you derive value from new analytics? The industrial and consumer printing company 3D Systems is creating platform- and service-based business models that go beyond selling hardware and consumables. How would recombining the components of your business give rise to new opportunities? How could the data you generate enable old and new customers to add value?

Consider new value-capture modes

Chances are that digitization will deflate some of your old models but will also create interesting new opportunities. SAP's cloud efforts allow it to charge customers for only the features they use, enhancing its ability to acquire new customers. Could you do a better job of tracking the actual value your business creates for others? Could you do a better job of monetizing that value, through either value-based pricing or outcomes-based models?

Use software to extend the boundaries of what you do

Digital transformation does not mean that your company will only sell software, but it will shift the capability base so that expertise in software development becomes increasingly important. And it won't render all traditional skills obsolete. Your existing capabilities and customer relationships are the foundations for new opportunities. Invest in software-related skills that complement what you have, but make sure you retain those critical foundations. Don't jettison your mechanical engineering wizards—couple them with some bright software developers so that you can do a better job of creating and extracting value.

New Structure and New Risks

Outcomes-based business models create new dependencies and risks as well as revenue opportunities. You will depend on the ability of your customers to operate successfully, and you'll be sensitive to the same economic trends and potential shocks that affect them.

GE is going to absorb a lot of business risk for its customers, but it has the financial understanding and capabilities to manage that risk. Smaller players will need to reach out to the financial sector for some carefully considered ways to cope with potential downsides.

The new ubiquity of digital technology and connectivity will have profound implications for the economy at large. The fortunes of Fairfield, Connecticut, where GE is based, will increasingly be tied to the weather at a wind farm in Germany, or to the operating efficiency of an airline headquartered in Abu Dhabi. Pressure on regulatory bodies will increase, and traditional institutions—from Fanny Mae to the U.S. Food and Drug Administration—may be unable to keep up. Inadequate regulation and a lack of transparency in financial instruments and institutions drove the global economy off a cliff in 2007–2008. In a world in which complex relationships across companies and industry segments may not always be understood, let alone transparent, something similar could occur. Booms and busts may become sharper and more violent. Furthermore, risks will be increasingly difficult to identify and manage, making busts harder to predict.

But no opportunity comes without risks, which are best handled with awareness and transparency. Individual investors, companies, and institutions should work to understand new assets, new connections, and new dependencies. Institutions should ensure that connections are transparent and that the powerful are held accountable for the impact of their decisions. Our hope is that this wave of opportunity will couple enthusiasm with reason. If the potential downsides are managed well, the short- and long-term rewards will be dramatic.

Originally published in November 2014. Reprint R1411D

About the Contributors

ETHAN BERNSTEIN is an assistant professor of business administration in the organizational behavior unit at Harvard Business School and the author of "The Transparency Paradox" (*Administrative Quarterly*, June 2012). Twitter: @ethanbernstein

MARCUS BUCKINGHAM provides performance management tools and training to organizations. He is the author of *StandOut 2.0: Assess Your Strengths, Find Your Edge, Win at Work* (Harvard Business Review Press, 2015) and several best-selling books.

RICHARD D'AVENI is the Bakala Professor of Strategy at Dartmouth College's Tuck School of Business.

HEIDI K. GARDNER is a distinguished fellow at the Center on the Legal Profession and a lecturer on law at Harvard Law School. She was previously on the Organizational Behavior faculty at Harvard Business School.

ASHLEY GOODALL is the director of leader development at Deloitte Services LP, based in New York.

REBECCA HOMKES is a fellow at London Business School's Centre for Management Development and a fellow at the London School of Economics Centre for Economic Performance.

MARCO IANSITI is the David Sarnoff Professor of Business Administration at Harvard Business School, where he heads the Technology and Operations Management Unit and the Digital Initiative. Twitter: @marcoiansiti and @digHBS

HERMINIA IBARRA is the Cora Chaired Professor of Leadership and Learning and a professor of organizational behavior at INSEAD. She is the author of *Act Like a Leader, Think Like a Leader* (Harvard Business Review Press, February 2015).

KARIM R. LAKHANI is an associate professor of business administration at HBS and principal investigator of the NASA Tournament Lab at Harvard University's for Quantitative Social Science. Twitter: @klakhani and @digHBS

WILLIAM LAZONICK is a professor of economics at the University of Massachusetts Lowell, the codirector of its Center for Industrial Competitiveness, and the president of the Academic-Industry Research Network. His book *Sustainable Prosperity in the New Economy? Business Organization and High-Tech Employment in the United States* (W.E. Upjohn Institute, 2009) won the 2010 Schumpeter Prize.

GREG LINDSAY is a contributing writer at *Fast Company* who is working on a book about serendipity and the intersection of social networks in physical space.

JENNIFER MAGNOLFI is an R&D consultant who focuses on programmable habitats and integrating the effects of coworking in the design and management of high-tech work environments.

JIM MANZI is the founder and chairman of Applied Predictive Technologies, which provides software for designing and analyzing business experiments.

KATHERINE L. MILKMAN is the James G. Campbell Jr. Assistant Professor of Operations and Information Management at the University of Pennsylvania's Wharton School. She is the coauthor (with Jack B. Soll and John W. Payne) of "A User's Guide to Debiasing," a chapter in *The Wiley Blackwell Handbook of Judgment and Decision Making,* forthcoming in 2015.

JOHN W. PAYNE is the Joseph J. Ruvane Jr. Professor of Business Administration at Duke University's Fuqua School of Business. He is the coauthor (with Jack B. Soll and Katherine L. Milkman) of "A User's Guide to Debiasing," a chapter in *The Wiley Blackwell Handbook of Judgment and Decision Making,* forthcoming in 2015.

JACK B. SOLL is an associate professor of management at Duke University's Fuqua School of Business. He is the coauthor (with Katherine L. Milkman and John W. Payne) of "A User's Guide to Debiasing," a chapter in *The Wiley Blackwell Handbook of Judgment and Decision Making,* forthcoming in 2015.

CHARLES SULL is a cofounder of and a partner at Charles Thames Strategy Partners.

DONALD SULL is a senior lecturer at the MIT Sloan School of Management and the author, with Kathleen M. Eisenhardt, of *Simple Rules: How to Thrive in a Complex World* (Houghton Mifflin Harcourt, 2015).

STEFAN THOMKE is the William Barclay Harding Professor of Business Administration at Harvard Business School.

BEN WABER is the president and CEO of Sociometric Solutions, a management services firm, and a visiting scientist at the MIT Media Lab.

Index

New Ideas and Resources to Help You Achieve Even More with
Harvard Business Review

EASIER, SMARTER, PERSONALIZED

As a business executive, you are called upon to lead; *Harvard Business Review* **provides the tools to keep you ahead, including the beautifully redesigned HBR.org. Imagine ...**

- On-demand access to more than 4,000 articles, interviews, features, and ideas in HBR.org's reimagined archive.

- Just-published articles *on topics you choose* rushed to your personalized My Library

- Seamless sharing of content with your colleagues.

Now, don't just imagine it. Employ it!

TO SEE ALL A SUBSCRIPTION INCLUDES, GO TO:
hbr.org/subscribe

The most important management ideas all in one place.

We hope you enjoyed this HBR's 10 Must Reads book. Now, you can get even more with HBR's 10 Must Reads Boxed Set. From books on leadership and strategy to managing yourself and others, this 6-book collection delivers articles on the most essential business topics to help you succeed.

HBR's 10 Must Reads Series

The HBR's 10 Must Reads Series is the definitive collection of ideas and best practices on our most sought-after topics from the best minds in business.

- The Essentials
- Leadership
- Strategy
- Managing People
- Managing Yourself
- Collaboration
- Communication
- Making Smart Decisions
- Teams
- Innovation
- Strategic Marketing
- Change Management